The One Who Listens

THE ONE WHO LISTENS

A Book of Prayer

MICHAEL HOLLINGS
and
ETTA GULLICK

MOREHOUSE-BARLOW CO.
New York

MOREHOUSE-BARLOW CO., INC.
14 East 41st St., New York, N.Y. 10017
SBN 0-8192-4037-0
Printed in the United States of America

CONTENTS

I

HEARING THE ONE
WHO LISTENS

We human beings are a mixture of complexity and simplicity; we get torn between human cravings which are material and earthbound, and human cravings which are spiritual and do not 'end on earth'.

How are we to develop and harmonise the whole of us, taking into account all the varieties of desire in our nature? The simple answer is to live to the fullest the human life we have. It is not an answer which carries us much further; but it is true all the same.

At a time of doubt and disbelief, when even religion is preaching secularisation, there is also a counter-movement, the driving force of which is man's sheer need for God. Where shall we find him? Is he to be found at all? How shall we find him?

It may seem mad to make such a statement today. However, if you look more closely at the world around you, you may well see signs.

The reason for this book is that in the fulness of human life, the way lies inward in an existence widely called *Prayer*. I say 'widely' because in the end it is co-existent with the whole of living. But unfortunately it is often narrowed down and misunderstood and becomes an occasional exercise, even among so-called religious people.

There are many ways of talking about prayer. Probably all of them are inadequate or emphasise a particular aspect. It would be as well, therefore, to look at them a little, not only so that we can see what approach may help us personally, but that we may understand better how each can limit us, or even lead us on the wrong path. I therefore set out here certain suggested or well-known descriptions, but by no means try to be exhaustive. Call prayer what you will, so long as you live it!

Talking to God

A simple, personalised expression, which appeals to the common factor of speech in us. It includes many basic concepts such as asking, praising, thanking. It uses our minds as well as our tongues. It seems to coincide with a real need, which could be said to be linked emotionally with joy, sorrow, fear, need, pain, illness, anticipation, love, gratitude, and so on—but which is so deep-rooted in man that social developments and even many direct attempts have not so far eradicated it. In real crisis, even today, there can be only a minority who do not utter something into the unknown! There is also through this process a possibility of growing somehow 'closer' to the 'One who listens'. The defect of such an emphasis is that it does not go far enough and tends to perpetuate the sense of God as an object to be addressed, a distant figure, outside, detached, to be approached. Whereas He is with us, within us, and we are to grow in this sense of closeness.

Dialogue with God

This is an extension of the former. Prayer has been described as 'being alone in a room talking to someone who isn't there'. It is, however, important to establish in our minds the sense of the 'two way' dimension in prayer. Dialogue is therefore more expressive than 'talking to', but the problem about it is that of the second voice in the dialogue, the come back from God. This is not 'audible' in the ordinary sense; rather it is 'experienced over a period of time'. It is not altogether unlike the effect which emerges through the listening relationship of a client and a psychotherapist.

Thinking about God

Here the *mind* is given more prominence. The mind, like talking, is common to all of us, and so very useful as a way into prayer. Each of us knows that we all think about ourselves and other people and the things of the world. We may not personally be very good, or very deep in our thinking, but unless we are so-called 'mentally deficient', we must accept that we have minds, and these can think, and therefore they can think about God, if he exists. There is no escape by saying: 'That is beyond me'.

Of course it is, but this should be a challenge and not a deterrent. If God exists, his creatures must be in touch with him. But he is spirit, so a bit abstract for some of us; to try to use a more abstract way will help, if we can manage it. But in Christianity and some other religions, it is not all abstract. We can also think about Christ or the prophets or the saints.

Often this is called *meditation*. This in itself frightens people, because they sincerely believe such an exercise is beyond them. *It is not*. We all meditate, though not always on God. It may be on the beauty of a picture or a piece of scenery; on the excellence of a good meal; on the virtues of tea over coffee; the merits of one footballer, or the teams which will win on Saturday; thoughts about a new hat, what to call the baby, the deepening of love of a fiancée and so on. But it is more personal if it is centring on the knowledge and love of a person; it is more spiritual if it is centred on the knowledge and love of God.

The advantages of this 'thinking about' are that we deepen our understanding of the one we are thinking about; we gather more of the excellence of God, we should then appreciate more, grow more interested in, and so find ourselves being led more into love. The disadvantages remain as with talking . . . we may tend to keep God as an object outside. And when we begin to work with our minds, there is an endless possibility of getting involved in theological speculation and even intellectual games, rather than growing in admiration, awe and love.

4

Finally, it is easy to allow ourselves to be confined within the limit of our own thought rather than opening to the presence of the infinite God.

Reflection

This is similar to thinking about, but it can be helpful to realise that we think very widely, and are subject to varying distractions. But we are involved with living, and God is not disconnected from our living. Therefore when we are musing about life, friends and happenings, we are not thereby cut off from God, but can be doing it openly with him. To sit quietly, having turned one's heart to God, and just let things flow through various levels of our consciousness is not wrong or negative, but can be very helpful and relaxing and developing.

Relationship with God

This idea is linked with person. It uses human relationship as a basis to work along, so that as with this human form conversation, knowledge, understanding and so on grow into intimacy and love. The human man/woman, person-to-person relationship grows through talking to and being with another, until there flowers something in the true depth of being which is inexpressible in words; it is LOVE in capital letters. We all know the awkwardness of a first meeting, the searching for topics, the shifting from foot to foot. I hope we all know too how this develops as we are easier together, as words become less necessary, because we know intuitively, understand feeling without speech. Then silence grows; just being close matters; we look at, we sense, we anticipate, we . . . well, we love.

With God, these same ideas work, especially perhaps in relating through Christ, who was himself a man. To study the Gospels is to study the relationship growing up between Christ and his disciples with varying degrees of success. Much spirituality has been developed along these lines with transference of the relationship to one between Christ and the person at prayer. This can form a way which is real and readily understandable to most people.

The disadvantages may lie in the likelihood of continuing on a level which is too imaginative and centred on the humanity of Christ rather than on his divinity. Also, Christ and God are not normally present in a tangible form, which causes a credibility gap in the relationship for some people, and we could not go so far as to say that the conversation and relationship are exactly the same 'man with man' and 'man with God'. The visual aids, the tangible presence, the come-back from the other frequently or normally seem to be absent in the God-relationship. They are not in fact absent because he is absent, but because he is spirit . . . but this at the time does not mean much!

Practising the presence of God

This sounds as if it specified a particular activity, which is carried out throughout the day and which begins at least with *Practice*—that is with the human endeavour to become aware of God in all our waking moments. Discipline is essential in all relationship, not least with God. Here it is emphasised in concentration and perseverance, because it is only in this way that prayer becomes a habit, and it is only when it is a habit that it becomes an effective power in spreading awareness of God through all our living. It should be noted also that it is more spiritual and should not depend too much on our images.

Growth in awareness

The Eastern approach to prayer stresses something of the awakening to the reality of God as within—a basically different concept from the 'object outside' which follows more naturally from the Western approach. This idea therefore has two properties for the West. Firstly, it may immediately appear more attractive and secondly it could throw doubt on the validity of the approaches previously outlined. This would be a pity, because the two are not necessarily exclusive.

Experience of God

'Be still and know that I am God'. Here 'know' is not the ordinary intellectual knowledge. It is what I can best express as a living experience; something realised more deeply than simply through the mind. It is like the experience of a person who suddenly 'knows' that he or she is 'in love'; how did it happen? I can't quite say, but there it is—a something, a loving. I suppose the biggest and most important aspect is that in this realisation is the knowledge that God is working in me. God loves me.

Having gone so far, what is this all about?

The One who listens is God. He is always with us.

Hearing is another way of saying experiencing or something like that; we have to listen so as to know, to learn to be responsive to God in prayer and in our whole living, for this is the importance of prayer in our lives.

May I make a personal statement? I have not always prayed, or even always believed. But coming through the past rapidly changing twenty-five years of world development, I 'discovered' prayer at the end of World War II, and swiftly learned that it is as essential to Christian living as is the air I breathe to ordinary living. With me, it was not always so, but I was fortunate enough to be shown by another person. Once I had 'seen', it was obvious, and has remained so.

The way has not all been either easy or hard. It can be grey, empty, painfully empty. Equally it can be stunningly lovely, peaceful, tender, absorbing; it can compel and flood with love in a way I cannot begin to write down.

In humility, I want to say that having experienced a tiny measure of God's infinite love—yes, experienced—I want desperately badly to awaken the possibility in others if in any way I can. This book may be one way. It tries through the expression of other people to begin and then move forward and inward by *realising* in growing silence the deep mystery of God's working and living in each of us. The sections show some sense of growth, and a brief word at each point shows a little of what that particular experience may be.

Now, here are a few points to begin with and to return to:

Prayer needs two—God and yourself.

Normally, vocal prayer continues throughout life.

Every human being is made by God 'for Himself', able to experience Him. You are one of these.

Growth is for everyone, not just a select few.

But growth demands time, energy, openness and generosity.

You really need to find a guide to help along the way.

You are in the world. Prayer does not take you out of the world. It makes you aware of the needs of the world.

Prayer will drive you to desire to supply those needs yourself.

Prayer is a whole lifetime of living and loving. It will cost your heart and your life, and it's worth it!

Prayer has to do with God. God is love. God loves you. You must love God, for 'love is repaid by love alone'.

9

The beginning

To begin to pray, or to carry on from where you are, you must believe in prayer, and you must be prepared to give up some of yourself in terms of time and effort. It will not be all easy, or all difficult. It will often be boring and seem 'not worth while', a waste of time. But you must keep on. Daily regularity is of the essence. Persevere for however long God may allow until there is a breakthrough. It is not easy to do more than say 'keep on', because it will come, but I cannot explain how. In God's time, you will be flooded with a 'sense' of it all. No one can teach you this, but you can experience it from God.

You must take down your defences, or allow them to be taken down. You must accept entering into darkness, with the act of faith that this darkness is creative. With Christ, with God, you must be stripped defenceless.

It is your contact with God in Christ, your being in his presence or company which enables him to infuse you with himself, with love, and which draws forth love from you in return.

Whatever means you use, or allow to be used in you, the ultimate goal is union of yourself with God, a union of love so closely complete that you can say with St. Paul: 'I live now not I, but Christ lives in me', and also: 'My life is hid with Christ in God'.

Psychologically we each need someone who will listen to us. Such a human person is not easy to find, though deep relationships provide this atmosphere of mutual listening, in love. If you can accept God as 'the One who listens', then talking to him about yourself (and everything and everyone in your life) makes sense. But it also makes sense to learn how you listen to him without just chattering on. This learning is not all that easy, because we need to learn to still ourselves; and we do not listen with the physical ear, but somehow in a way unknown, we become aware of the still small voice which 'speaks' to our own stillness . . . the voice of 'the One who listens'. Once you know or experience this, you listen as he listens—and it spreads to everything and continues always all the time, and this is when we can say that silence speaks to silence.

II

DAY AND NIGHT PRAYERS

To have real meaning, prayer must be woven into daily life, be part of the fabric of living. This has led many people to adopt a routine practice of morning and night prayer.

Speaking honestly and simply, one of the most difficult aspects of prayer is just getting down to it regularly. But I do not know personally of any holy person in history or whom I have met in my own experience who was haphazard or casual about prayer. For them it has been and is vital.

This does not mean that they found it easy. After all, they were ordinary men and women like ourselves; the danger of reading the life of a saint is that authors tend to highlight the ecstasies and pass over the day by day slog. Saints usually recognised that if they did not fix themselves in a 'rule' of living, their spiritual life might not have the right climate for growth. Into this rule it seemed natural to put the two poles of morning and evening, the beginning and end of the day, for prayer.

The examples which follow are from various sources, fairly widely spread to show something of the possibility. You may find one here and there

12

which is helpful now, or next year. Take them and use them as best you can—slowly, thoughtfully. But in the long run, God wants you to speak to him in your own words, not someone else's. Use what comes into your head, let out what is in your heart, breathe your love, your hope, your faith. It can be that out of what you pray here you will be encouraged to go on simply. It does not really matter *what* you say. God wants you, and you need and want the listening one.

Morning

O Lord, grant me to greet the coming day in peace. Help me in all things to rely upon thy holy will. In every hour of the day reveal thy will to me. Bless my dealings with all who surround me. Teach me to treat all that comes to me throughout the day with peace of soul, and with firm conviction that thy will governs all. In all my deeds and words guide my thoughts and feelings. In unforeseen events let me not forget that all are sent by thee. Teach me to act firmly and wisely, without embittering and embarrassing others. Give me strength to bear the fatigue of the coming day with all that it shall bring. Direct my will, teach me to pray, pray thou thyself in me.

Metropolitan Philaret of Moscow (died 1867)

O Lord, when I awake and day begins
   waken me to thy presence;
   waken me to thy indwelling;
   waken me to inward sight of thee,

13

and speech with thee
and strength from thee;
that all my earthly walk may waken into song
and my spirit leap up to thee all day,
all ways.

Eric Milner-White

Thou who sendest forth the light, createst the morning, makest the sun to rise on the good and the evil, enlighten the blindness of our minds with the knowledge of the truth: lift thou up the light of thy countenance upon us, that in thy light we may see light, and, at the last, in the light of grace and in the light of glory.

Lancelot Andrewes (1555-1626)

Help us this day, O God, to serve thee devoutly, and the world busily. May we do our work wisely, give succour secretly, go to our meat appetitely, sit thereat discreetly, arise temperately, please our friends duly, go to our bed merrily, and sleep surely; for the joy of our Lord, Jesus Christ.

Anonymous Medieval

O God, our Father, help us all through this day so to live that we may bring help to others, credit to ourselves and to the name we bear, and joy to those that love us, and to thee.
Help us to be,
    Cheerful when things go wrong;

Persevering when things are difficult;
Serene when things are irritating.
Enable us to be,
Helpful to those in difficulties;
Kind to those in need;
Sympathetic to those whose hearts are sore and
sad.
Grant that,
Nothing may make us lose our tempers;
Nothing may take away our joy;
Nothing may ruffle our peace;
Nothing may make us bitter towards any man.
So grant that through all this day all with whom
we work, and all those whom we meet, may see in
us the reflection of the Master, whose we are, and
whom we seek to serve. This we ask for thy love's
sake.

William Barclay

Grant us, O Lord, to pass this day in gladness
and peace, without stumbling and without stain;
that, reaching the eventide victorious over all
temptations, we may praise thee, the eternal God,
who art blessed, and dost govern all things, world
without end.

Mozarabic Liturgy

O Lord, our heavenly Father, almighty and everlasting God, who hast safely brought us to the
Beginning of this day: defend us in the same with
thy mighty power, and grant that this day we fall

into no sin, neither run into any kind of danger; but that all our doings may be ordered by thy governance, to do always that which is righteous in thy sight, through Jesus Christ our Lord. Amen.

Book of Common Prayer

The day returns and brings us the petty round of irritating concerns and duties. Help us to play the man, help us to perform them with laughter and kind faces, let cheerfulness abound with industry. Give us to go blithely on our business this day, bring us to our resting beds weary and content and undishonoured, and grant us in the end the gift of peace.

R. L. Stevenson (1850-1894)

Lord, as we go to our work this day, help us to take pleasure therein. Show us clearly what our duty is, help us to be faithful in doing it. May all we do be well done, fit for thine eye to see. Give us enthusiasm to attempt, patience to perform. When we cannot love our work, may we think of it as thy task, and make what is unlovely beautiful through loving service, for thy name's sake.

George Dawson (1821-1876)

Noon

Blessed Saviour, who at this hour didst hang upon the cross stretching forth thy loving arms,

16

grant that all mankind may look unto thee and be saved.

Lord Jesus, who didst stretch out thine arms of love on the hard wood of the cross, that all men might come within the reach of thy saving embrace, clothe us in thy spirit, that we, stretching forth our hands in loving labour for others, may bring those who know thee not to the knowledge and love of thee, who with the Father and the Holy Ghost livest and reignest one God.

Night

Into thy hands, O Lord and Father, we commend our souls and our bodies, our parents and our homes, friends and servants, neighbours and kindred, our benefactors and brethren departed, all thy people faithfully believing, and all who need thy pity and protection. Enlighten us with thy holy grace, and suffer us never more to be separated from thee, who art one God in Trinity, God everlasting.

O Lord my God, I thank thee
that thou has brought this day to a close;
I thank thee for giving me rest

in body and soul.
Thy hand has been over me
and has guarded and preserved me.
Forgive my lack of faith
and any wrong that I have done today,
and help me to forgive all who have wronged us.
Let me sleep in peace under thy protection,
and keep me from all the temptations of darkness.
Into thy hands I commend my loved ones
and all who dwell in this house;
I commend to thee my body and soul.
O God, thy holy name be praised.

Dietrich Bonhoeffer (1906-1945)

Be present, O merciful God, and protect us through the silent hours of the night, that we who are wearied by the changes and chances of this fleeting world may repose upon thy eternal changelessness, through the everlasting Christ our Lord.

Gelasian Sacramentary

Eternal and ever-blessed God, we give thee thanks, as the day comes to an end, for those who mean so much to us, and without whom life could never be the same.

We thank thee for those to whom we can go at any time and never feel a nuisance.

We thank thee for those to whom we can go when we are tired, knowing that they have, for the weary feet, the gift of rest.

We thank thee for those with whom we can talk, and keep nothing back, knowing that they will not laugh at our dreams or mock our failures.

We thank thee for those in whose presence it is easier to be good.

We thank thee for those in whose company joys are doubly dear, and sorrow's bitterness is soothed.

We thank thee for those who by their warning counsel and their rebuke have kept us from mistakes we might have made, and sins we might have committed.

And above all we thank thee for Jesus, the pattern of our lives, the Lord of our hearts, and the Saviour of our souls.

Accept this our thanksgiving, and grant us to-night a good night's rest; through Jesus Christ our Lord.

William Barclay

Save us, O Lord, while waking, and guard us while sleeping, that when we wake, we may watch with Christ, and when we sleep we may rest in peace.

Roman Breviary

Glory to thee, my God, this night
For all the blessings of the light;
Keep me, O keep me, King of kings,
Beneath thine own almighty wings.
Forgive me, Lord, for thy dear Son,

The ill that I this day have done,
That with the world, myself, and thee,
I, ere I sleep, at peace may be.
  Teach me to live, that I may dread
The grave as little as my bed;
Teach me to die, that so I may
Rise glorious at the awful day.
  Praise God, from whom all blessings flow,
Praise him, all creatures here below,
Praise him above, ye heavenly host,
Praise Father, Son and Holy Ghost.

Thomas Ken (1637-1711)

O God, I thank you for life and being, and for all the blessings of the past day; for the love I have received and given, for all the kindnesses that I have received from others, for thy grace going before me and following after me. Above all I thank thee for him through whom I know thy love and receive thy grace, even Jesus Christ, my Lord and Saviour.

George Appleton

Almighty Father, who in thy divine mercy dost cover the earth with the curtain of night that all the weary may rest, grant to us and to all men rest in thee this night. Let thy grace, we beseech thee, comfort and support all that are to spend it in sorrow, in loneliness, affliction, or in fear. We commend into thy hands ourselves, with all who are dear to us. Strengthen and confirm thy faithful

people, arouse the careless, relieve the sick, give
peace to the dying that thy holy name may be
glorified in Christ Jesus, thy Son, our Lord.

H. Stobart

O Lord our God, what sins I have this day
committed in word, deed, or thought, forgive me,
for thou art gracious, and thou lovest all men.
Grant me peaceful and undisturbed sleep, send me
thy guardian angel to protect and guard me from
every evil, for thou art the guardian of our souls and
bodies, and to thee we ascribe glory, to the Father
and the Son and the Holy Ghost, now and for ever
and unto the ages of ages.

Russian Orthodox prayer

From all my lame defeats and oh! much more
From all the victories that I seemed to score;
From cleverness shot forth on thy behalf,
At which, while angels weep, the audience laugh;
From all my proofs of thy divinity,
Thou, who wouldst give no sign, deliver me.
Thoughts are but coins. Let me not trust instead
Of thee, their thin-worn image of their head.
From all my thoughts, even from my thoughts of
    thee,
O thou fair silence, fall, and set me free.
Lord of the narrow gate and needle's eye,
Take from me all my trumpery, lest I die.

C. S. Lewis

I will lay me down in peace
and take my rest:
For it is thou Lord, only,
That makest me to dwell in safety.
Into thy hands O Lord,
I commend my spirit,
For thou hast redeemed me,
O Lord, thou God of truth.

Compline

O Lord, support us all the day long, until the
shadows lengthen and the evening comes, and the
busy world is hushed, and the fever of life is over,
and our work is done. Then, Lord, in thy mercy
grant us a safe lodging, and a holy rest, and peace
at the last; through Jesus Christ our Lord.

*Attributed to J. H. Newman though it may
have been earlier in origin*

God that madest earth and heaven,
    Darkness and light,
Who the day for toil hast given,
    For rest the night;
Guard us waking, guard us sleeping,
    And when we die:
May we in thy mighty keeping
    All peaceful lie.

R. Heber (1783-1826)

III

FOR MOODS, CRISES, JOYS, SUFFERINGS AND ALL LIFE'S EVENTS

Much of life is humdrum, but we all meet crisis, pain and loss, as we also meet thrilling excitements and joys. Some people think it hypocritical or unfair to turn to God in a crisis; yet this is the very time when those most unused to prayer want to turn to someone—someone more powerful than a doctor or a priest, and differently involved from someone dearly loved. We are very alone in crisis.

Now, it would be better if prayer was more regular—if you were living in a 'climate' of prayer. Apart from anything else, you would find that the depression or pain and so on felt different; they are just as intense, but not quite so lonely, perhaps.

Christ came for the sick and the imprisoned, the poor and sinners. The cry of need is in all humanity—and it is listened to by God. No matter who you are, try to pray at such times as these. If you cannot find the words, see how others have poured out their hearts—and in the depths as you may be, remember that Christ was truly a man, that he was deserted by friends, was tired, wept at ingratitude and wept at the death of a friend.

So much does our mood change that we may want to prolong our tale of woe, we may feel only able to utter the single word 'help' or 'Lord'. In joy we may want to sing, or shout 'Alleluia', or sigh. Here the way is open for the enormous variety in us and our need or our expression of love.

GENERAL

Before prayer

O Lord take away all coldness, all wanderings of the thoughts, and fix our souls upon thee and thy love, O merciful Lord and Saviour, in this our hour of prayer.

Edward W. Benson (1829-1896)

Give me grace, O my Father, to be utterly ashamed of my own reluctance. Rouse me from sloth and coldness, and make me desire thee with my whole heart. Teach me to love meditation, sacred reading, and prayer. Teach me to love that which must engage my mind for all eternity.

John Henry Newman (1801-1890)

Holy Jesus, give me the gift and spirit of prayer; and do thou by thy gracious intercession supply my ignorance, and passionate desires, and imperfect choices; procuring and giving me such returns of favour which may support my needs, and serve the ends of religion and the Spirit, which thy wisdom chooses, and thy passion hath purchased, and thy grace loves to bestow upon all thy saints and servants.

Jeremy Taylor (1613-1667)

For thy coming, Lord, we pray,
But let it be some other day.
On thy return our hopes are set;
Thy will be done, but not just yet.

Osbert Lancaster

Help me to be human
God, help me to be truly human.
Help me to be able to appreciate
and bring out the best in everyone around me.
Help me to be able to give of the best in myself.
    Many people think that to be human is
to make mistakes, to hate, to be imperfect.
But this is not true.
When Jesus was on earth,
he showed us the way
in which we should live.
    Man is not like the animal.
He does not exist, he lives.
He does not feed, he eats.
He does not mate, he loves.
He does not breed, he co-creates.
    You have created man,
so that he is capable
to appreciate consciously
all the gifts
that you have given him.
Lord, help me to appreciate all
that you have given me.
Help me to be truly human.

'*Lord, make me truly human*', *Teenagers'*
prayers from Salisbury, Rhodesia

For guidance

We beseech thee, O Lord, to enlighten our minds and to strengthen our wills, that we may know what we ought to do, and be enabled to do it, through the grace of thy most Holy Spirit, and for the merits of thy Son, Jesus Christ our Lord.

William Bright (1824-1901)

Guide me, teach me, strengthen me, till I become such a person as thou wouldst have me be; pure and gentle, truthful and high-minded, brave and able, courteous and generous, dutiful and useful.

Charles Kingsley (1819-1875)

For knowledge of God

Almighty God, give us wisdom to perceive thee, intellect to understand thee, diligence to seek thee, patience to wait for thee, eyes to behold thee, a heart to meditate upon thee, and life to proclaim thee, through the power of the spirit of our Lord Jesus Christ.

Attributed to Saint Benedict (480-543)

For doing God's will

Dear Lord, quieten my spirit and fix my thoughts on thy will, that I may see what thou wouldst have done, and contemplate its doing without self-consciousness or inner excitement, without haste and without delay, without fear of other people's judgements or anxiety about success, knowing only that it is thy will and therefore must be done quietly, faithfully and lovingly, for in thy will alone is our peace.

George Appleton

For dependence on God

Grant, O God, that amidst all the discouragements, difficulties and dangers, distress and darkness of this mortal life, I may depend upon thy mercy, and on this build my hopes, as on a sure foundation. Let thine infinite mercy in Christ Jesus deliver me from despair, both now and at the hour of death.

Thomas Wilson (1663-1755)

Before daily work

O Lord, renew our spirits and draw our hearts unto thyself, that our work may not be to us a burden, but a delight; and give us such a mighty love to thee as may sweeten our obedience. O let us not serve thee with the spirit of bondage as slaves, but with cheerfulness and gladness, delighting ourselves in thee and rejoicing in thy work.

Benjamin Jenks (1647-1724)

Before study

O God, who hast ordained that whatever is to be desired, should be sought by labour, and who, by thy blessing, bringest honest labour to good effect, look with mercy upon my studies and endeavours. Grant me, O Lord, to desire only what is lawful and right; and afford me calmness of mind, and steadiness of purpose, that I may so do thy will in this short life, as to obtain happiness in the world to come; for the sake of Jesus Christ our Lord.

Samuel Johnson (1709-1784)

MOODS AND CRISES

In coldness of heart

O my sweet Saviour Christ, which in thine undeserved love towards mankind so kindly wouldst suffer the painful death of the cross, suffer me not to be cold nor lukewarm in love again towards thee.

Saint Thomas More (1478-1535)

In sadness

Oh God! Behold my grief and care. I would serve thee with a glad heart and cheerful countenance, but I cannot do it. However much I struggle against my sadness, I am too weak for this sore conflict. Help me in my weakness, O thou mighty God.

S. Scheretz

When dissatisfied with self

To thee, O Jesus, thou peace of the troubled heart, I come! Save me from myself. Shine into my heart with thy life and love. Melt away all cold distrust. Take away all sin; and make me like to thyself, for thy love and kindness' sake, O Lord!

W. Boyd Carpenter (1841-1918)

When complaining

If I am to complain, let me complain to Jesus fastened on his cross. But in thy presence, my Saviour, what have I to complain of? What are my sufferings compared with those thou bearest without complaining? I might perhaps convince my fellow-man that I am unjustly afflicted, but in thy presence, Lord, I cannot, for my sins are known to thee. Thou knowest my sufferings are far less than I deserve. And since all my afflictions proceed from thee, reproach not my afflictions, not my wrongs, but myself and my own want of patience. To they I come; give me strength, and hearten me to suffer in silence; as once thou didst thyself.

Blessed Claude de la Colombière

When anxious

Set free, O Lord, my soul from all restlessness and anxiety; give me that peace and power which flow from thee; keep me in all perplexities and distresses, in all fears and faithlessness; that so upheld by thy power and stayed on the rock of the faithfulness, I may through storm and stress abide in thee, through Christ Jesus our Lord.

'New Every Morning'

In worry

O Lord, we know we very often worry about things that may never happen. Help us to live one day at a time, and to live it for you; for your name's sake.

Beryl Bye

In trouble or danger

O God help me to remember when I am troubled or in danger that neither death nor life, nor angels, nor principalities, nor powers, nor things present, nor things to come, nor height, nor depth, nor any other creature is able to separate me from your love which is in Christ Jesus our Lord.

Romans, Chapter 8, verses 38-39

When hurt

O Lord, my God, grant that when I am hurt, I may stand before thee for healing, when self-willed, come to thee for self-noughting, when worried, lay my burden at thy feet and find serenity and love.

George Appleton

Lord, I am very hurt, and you have done nothing to help! It was a lovely day and I was looking forward to seeing him. I hoped our love would grow, but he brought a friend and they were only concerned with their problems. I was forgotten. I don't want to see him again. Please stop me from feeling like that about you too. Don't let me turn from you in my hurtness. But help and comfort me and teach me how to love as you do, understandingly and forgivingly, Lord.

Anonymous

When jealous

O Lord, stop me from feeling jealous. Help me to share in my friends' and enemies' successes, and not to be jealous when they are praised and thanked and I am not. Live in me, O Lord, and work through me, and let me see my successes as yours that I may be one with you as you are with the Father.

Help me too not to be jealous when those I love seem to love others more than me, but make me love you more and to find you increasingly in all men.

Etta Gullick

Lord, I could wish him dead. Each time I'm just getting somewhere, he gets ahead of me. Each time a thought comes into my head, he utters it before I can find the words. Each time I make a new friend, he seems to take him up and leave me behind. Lord, I'm jealous of him, and I pity myself. I'm full of it and I can't get rid of that thought of him. I know he'll do it again, and I know you tell me I must love my enemy . . . and I can't . . . and yet, Lord, with your help I *will*. Help me, Lord.

Michael Hollings

She's charming, she's beautiful (though I won't admit it), she's more beautiful than I am, and more attractive to the men I know. Don't you see, Lord, that it is eating into me, this jealousy? I can't bear to watch her, I'm full of bitterness, self pity, the lot.

How I hate myself for hating her—Lord let me get out of this, and take her as a friend, and enjoy her success—yes, and learn to love her.

Anonymous

Lord, let this chalice pass—this irritation and jealousy and almost hatred—but not my will but yours be done.

Michael Hollings

When envious

Give me thy grace, O Lord, that I may never envy any good man's or woman's love because they do either love God and his people more than I. Make me to rejoice in other men's gifts, and not envy them, because they be better than mine; but rather to give thanks for them with all my heart, desiring that they be increased in them and in me.

'Christian Prayer' (1566)

When made a fool of

Smarting and humbled, I come to you. I have been exposed. Whether I have deserved it or not, I will try to avoid useless recriminations. Nor will I try to justify myself; excuses would almost certainly involve me in lying. Instruct me in humility, Lord, or I shall always be distracted by this kind of vulnerability. Let me not take my prestige too seriously, and above all let the fear of humiliation never prevent me from doing something I feel you want. Just as neither money nor health should have the final and absolute say in my decisions, so I beg that this particular brand of worldly wisdom which is equivocally called amour-propre may never be given the casting vote.

Hubert van Zeller, OSB

In failure

O God, whose blessed Son was despised and rejected of men, help us to accept our failures as real and necessary instructions in our pilgrimage toward freedom and wholeness in Jesus Christ our Saviour.

Robert Rodenmayer

In despair of self

O Lord God, I see my fellow men I know that I have a duty towards. I recognise the law and justice that would restrain my selfish instincts. I will keep from hurt, hatred, exploitation. But of myself, I cannot love them. Only if you give me love can I love. In despair of myself, O Trinity of love, I ask for love.

George Appleton

When troubled in mind

God, Father of Mercies, save me from the hell within me. I acknowledge thee, I adore and bless thee, whose throne is in heaven, with thy Blessed

Son and crucified Jesus, and thy Holy Spirit, and also, though thou slay me, yet will I trust in thee; I cannot think thou can hate and reject a poor soul that desires to love thee and cleave to thee, so long as I can hold by the skirts of thy garments, until thou violently shake me off; which I am confident thou wouldst not do, because thou art love and goodness itself and thy mercies endure for ever.

Robert Leighton (1611-1684)

In fear

O Lord, take my fear away from me. May I know with the prophet Isaiah that I never need fear because you are with me, and I need not be dismayed because you are my God. Let me realise in the depth of my being that I am in your hands, and that by trusting you, my fear is lost in you, because you care for me.

Etta Gullick

In time of temptation

Help me, Lord, or I shall perish. Lord Jesus, stiller of storms, bring peace to my soul. Lord Jesus, I want to please thee rather than to sin; and if I do not feel that I want to please thee, give me the grace to want to please thee. I *want* to want to please thee . . . and I do not want to sin.*

Hubert van Zeller, OSB

---

* And, by the time you have worked that out, with the grace of God and with any luck, you will have forgotten about the temptation.

When lonely

Show me how to approach my sense of being alone and cut off so that it may not be any longer a condition to be dreaded, but rather seen as a means to closer dependence upon you. Let my soul learn in solitude the lesson of your presence.

'A Book of Private Prayer'

When distracted

When the heart is hard and parched up, come upon me with a shower of mercy.

When grace is lost from life, come with a burst of song.

When tumultuous work raises its din on all sides shutting me out from beyond, come to me, my Lord of silence, with thy peace and rest.

When my beggarly heart sits crouched, shut up in a corner, break open the door, my king, and come with the ceremony of a king.

When desire blinds the mind with delusion and dust, O thou holy one, thou wakeful, come with thy light and thy thunder.

Rabindranath Tagore (1861-1941)

When in a bad mood

Lord, I know I am in a shocking state of mind. In a way I feel I ought not to be praying at all; I am far too disgruntled for recollection and generosity and good resolutions and all these things which are necessary to your service. But I know at the same time that it is better to try to pray than to merely give in and indulge in my poisonous humour. Possibly if I prayed more, I would be less at the mercy of these glooms. Lord, show me how to deal with myself when rebellion and bitterness well up in me, and make life seem far more of a burden than it is. Give me the strength to break myself in as I would a rebellious colt. Show me that the remedy lies in submission to you and not in wallowing in self. Lord, I accept, so far as possible, I spit out the venom which is in me, and I bow before your will. And thank you, Lord, I feel better now.

Hubert van Zeller, OSB

When Tired

I am tired, Lord,
too tired to think,
too tired to pray,
too tired to do anything.
Too tired,
drained of resources,
'labouring at the oars against a head wind,'
pressed down by a force as strong as the sea.
Lord of all power and might,
'your way was through the sea,
your path through the great waters',
calm my soul,
take control,
Lord of all power and might.

Rex Chapman

In old age

    See, Lord,
my coat hangs in tatters
like homespun, old, threadbare.
All that I had of zest,
all my strength
I have given in hard work
and kept nothing for myself.
Now
my poor head swings.
I offer up all the loneliness of my heart.
Dear God,
stiff on my thickened legs
I stand here before you,
your unprofitable servant.
Oh! of your goodness,
give me a gentle death.

'The prayer of the old horse'
Carmen Bernos de Gasztold

May Christ—Omega keep me always *young* 'to
the greater glory of God'.
    For
      old age comes from him
      old age leads on to him, and
      old age will touch me only in so far as he wills.
To be 'young' means to be hopeful, energetic,
smiling—and clear-sighted.
    May I accept death in whatever guise it may come
to me in Christ—Omega, that is within the process
of the development of life.

A smile (inward and outward) means facing with sweetness and gentleness whatever befalls me.

Jesus—Omega, grant me to *serve you*, to proclaim you, to glorify you, to make you manifest, to the very end through all the time that remains to me of life, and above all through my death.

Desperately, Lord Jesus, I commit to your care my last active years, and my death; do not let them impair or spoil the work I have so dreamed of achieving for you.

Teilhard de Chardin

In wakefulness

O Lord let me sleep! You have said that you will give your beloved sleep. I know you love me, please give me sleep. Or let me rest quietly in you and realize that I am sharing with you the sleeplessness of the starving, the lonely, the lost and the old who are so much worse off than I. Let me know that my wakefulness is not wasted but helps to make up what is lacking in your suffering.

Etta Gullick

In times of doubt regarding belief

In times of doubt and questionings, when our belief is perplexed by new learning, new teaching, new thought, when our faith is strained by creeds, by doctrines, by mysteries beyond our understanding, give us the faithfulness of learners and courage of believers in thee; give us boldness to examine and faith to trust in all truth; patience and insight to master difficulties; stability to hold fast our tradition with enlightened interpretation, to admit all fresh truth made known to us, and in times of trouble to grasp new knowledge really and to combine it loyally and honestly with the old; insight to refrain from stubborn rejection of new revelations and from hasty assurance that we are wiser than our fathers. Save us and help us, we humbly beseech thee, O Lord.

George Ridding (1828-1904)

When trying to understand doubts

Why should doubts come now of all times?
I have reasoned things out, and seen the issues clearly.
I have decided to have faith, and act in faith.
I have gladly given myself to you.

Why then these doubts?

Shouldn't they have disappeared when I made my decision?
Shouldn't that wave of great peace and joy, that that sense of destiny and fulfilment which came to me then, should not these have dug the roots of doubt out of my mind for good?

Or could it be that these doubts are drawing my attention to some part of my mind where there are problems which I haven't faced and dealt with yet?

Are they like a toothache which registers at some point remote from the actual source of the trouble?

—like pains in a leg which indicate an injury to the back?

If so, Lord, help me to trace the doubt to its real source. Help me to seek out the root causes of my doubt, and help me to do it fearlessly in the knowledge that I can do nothing against the truth:

that what is true will remain true, however radical my questioning may be.

Or are these doubts
just excuses which I provide for myself
(from the subconscious resources of hidden selfishness) in order not to do something which I know I ought to do but do not wish to do?

Or are these doubts reminders
sent by God himself
who wishes his children to be men of faith:
men for whom faith is not just assent, not just an act, but a continuing
lifelong
activity?

Thank you Lord for these doubts.
Teach me, through them, all that I need to know.
Make me, through them, all that I need to become.

Dick Williams

When worldly

We let the world overcome us, we live too much in continual fear of the chances and changes of mortal life, we let things go too much their own way, we try too much each to get what he can by his own selfish wits, without considering his neighbours.

We follow too much the ways and fashions of the day, doing and saying and thinking anything that comes uppermost, just because others do so around us. Guide, good Lord, to see your way and to follow your will.

Charles Kingsley (1819-1875)

SUFFERING

In sickness

My strength fails; I feel only weakness, irritation and depression. I am tempted to complain and to despair. What has become of the courage I was so proud of, and that gave me so much self-confidence? In addition to my pain, I have to bear the shame of my fretful feebleness. Lord, destroy my pride; leave it no resource. How happy I shall be if you can teach me by these terrible trials, that I am nothing, that I can do nothing, and that you are all!

François Fénelon (1631-1715)

Lord, let this sickness, like that of Lazarus, be unto the Father's glory and for the good of those who stand by. I must see to it that whatever I have to suffer is not wasted but is offered to the Father, and also that I do not give cause for disedification to those who have to wait on me. Inspire me during my illness at least to think of you occasionally: I do not want to make this time, so far as prayer is concerned, a blank. If my regular practices have to be abandoned, show me what new ones I may substitute. Give me, I pray you, a more vivid awareness of your presence, so as to make up for the kind of willed recollection which I try to maintain when I am well.

Hubert van Zeller, OSB

Lord, teach me the art of patience whilst I am well, and give me the use of it when I am sick. In that day either lighten my burden or strengthen my back. Make me, who so often in my health have discovered my weakness, presuming on my own strength, to be strong in my sickness when I rely solely on thy assistance.

Thomas Fuller (1608-1661)

The Lord gave, and the Lord hath taken away.

Job, Chapter 1, verse 21

Lord, you made your servant Job say this in the depth of his misfortunes. How kind you are to put these words in the mouth of a sinner like me. You gave me health and I forgot you. You take it away and I come back to you. What infinite compassion that God in order to give himself to me, takes away his gifts which I allowed to come between me and him. Lord, take away everything that is not you. All is yours. You are the Lord. Dispose everything, comforts, success, health. Take all the things that possess me instead of you that I may be wholly yours.

François Fénelon (1631-1715)

In pain

We ask thee not, O Lord, to rid us of pain; but grant in thy mercy that our pain may be free from waste, unfretted by rebellion against thy will, unsoiled by thought of ourselves, purified by love of our kind and ennobled by devotion to thy kingdom, through the mercies of thine only Son, our Lord.

Book of Common Prayer (1928)

When bereaved

O God, our only help in time of need, be close to me in my sorrow, in your mercy give me strength to keep going, and help me to trust you whatever happens and increase my love. Into your loving hands I commend myself and the soul of . . .; give us peace and rest in you.

Etta Gullick

When death approaches

O my most blessed and glorious creator, that hast fed me all my life long, and redeemed me from all evil; seeing it is thy merciful pleasure to take me out of this frail body, and to wipe away all tears from mine eyes, and all sorrows from my heart, I do with all humility and willingness consent and submit myself wholly unto thy sacred will. My most loving redeemer, into thy saving and everlasting arms I commend my spirit; I am ready, my dear Lord, and earnestly expect and long for thy good pleasure. Come quickly, and receive the soul of thy servant which trusteth in thee.

Henry Vaughan (1621-1695)

Father, into thy hands I commend my spirit.

Luke, Chapter 23, verse 46

PRAYERS FOR ...

For purity

Almighty God, unto whom all hearts be open, all desires known, and from whom no secrets are hid; cleanse the thoughts of our hearts by the inspiration of thy Holy Spirit, that we may perfectly love thee and worthily magnify thy holy name; through Christ our Lord.

Book of Common Prayer

Lord Jesus, you were a man; you had my eyes, my ears, my sense of touch and smell; you know my feelings of body and heart; you were like me in everything—except sin. But, Lord, were you never tempted by human beauty, the beauty you had created? Surely, anyhow, you understand how I feel now. How I long for what I should not have! Tempted as I am, help me not to sin.

Michael Hollings

Lord, I want her. I want her so badly, I ache all over, and it seems wrong, yet it doesn't seem wrong. And she wants me, I know. Give us both strength to love the right way.

Anonymous

Lord, I'm all alone, and so lonely. I know what it means to have the warmth of human love, the close touch of flesh to flesh. But I'm alone now. Help me not to wallow in my thoughts and imagination and desire, all alone. Get me out of this rut, Lord.

Michael Hollings

Oh God! It tears me apart saying 'no'. All my heart and my body cry out 'yes'. Must I say 'no'? Why, Lord, when you made this body and this desire and this beauty and this love must I say 'no'?

Michael Hollings

Jesus, because John says you loved him, you have been called a homosexual. Can you tell me, Lord, the right and the wrong; how to love and not lust? Can a man love a man and a woman a woman, yet not sin? Where does love and lust begin? I must know, Lord, because I must live. Give me strength and courage to go on loving and to truly live.

Anonymous

O eternal God, who has taught us by thy holy word that our bodies are the temples of thy Spirit, keep us we most humbly beseech thee temperate and holy in thought, word, and deed, that at the last we, with all the pure in heart, may see thee, and be made like unto thee in thy heavenly kingdom, through Christ our Lord.

Brooke Foss Westcott (1823-1901)

For humility

Dear Christ, teach us how to be humble. Teach us how to live as you did, respecting others however lowly, poor and unattractive they are. Teach us to do the humblest tasks the way you did, in unhurried quietness of mind, not thinking that we are fitted for more exciting duties. Teach us to see how unworthy we are of all the gifts that you have given us, and not to regard them as our right. O Lord may we see how small we are in comparison with you, and in realizing this forget our self-importance, and serve you and our brothers in true humbleness of heart.

Etta Gullick

For patience

When many are coming and going and there is little leisure, give us grace, O heavenly Father, to follow the example of our Lord Jesus Christ, who knew neither impatience of spirit nor confusion of work, but in the midst of his labours held communion with thee, and even upon earth was still in heaven; where he now reigneth with thee and the Holy Spirit world without end.

C. J. Vaughan (1816-1897)

For single-mindedness

Give us, O Lord, a steadfast heart, which no unworthy affection may drag downwards; give us an unconquered heart, which no tribulation can wear out; give us an upright heart, which no unworthy purpose may tempt aside. Bestow upon us also, O Lord our God, understanding to know thee, diligence to seek thee, wisdom to find thee, and a faithfulness that may finally embrace thee; through Jesus Christ our Lord.

Saint Thomas Aquinas (1225-1274)

For perseverance

Keep me, O Lord, while I tarry on this earth, in a daily serious seeking after thee and in a believing affectionate walking with thee; that when thou comest, I may be found not hiding my talent, nor yet asleep with my lamp unfurnished; but waiting and longing for my Lord, my glorious God, for ever and ever.

Richard Baxter (1615-1691)

For serenity

God grant me
the serenity to accept the things I cannot change,
the courage to change the things I can,
and the wisdom to distinguish the one from the other.

Reinhold Niebuhr

For trust

O God, the strength of those who walk with thee, without whom nothing is safe, nothing is tranquil, confirm in us the knowledge of thy presence, that, thou being our companion in the way, we may so deal with our anxieties that at length our hearts may find their rest in thee, through Jesus Christ our Lord.

J. W. Suter

You tell me to trust and obey, but I do not know how to, though I want to. Please show me how, for I am certain that it is only by trusting that I can have peace and joy. Let me believe in you and let me know you in some way so I may be able to trust. Help me to believe and drive away my unbelief, and give me your peace.

Etta Gullick

For courage

Let me not pray to be sheltered from dangers, but to be fearless in facing them;
Let me not beg for the stilling of my pain, but for the heart to conquer it.
Let me not look for allies in life's battlefield but to my own strength.
Let me not crave in anxious fear to be saved but hope for the patience to win my freedom.

Grant me that I may not be a coward, feeling your mercy in my success alone, but let me find the grasp of your hand in my failure.

Rabindranath Tagore (1861-1941)

For a sense of humour

Give us a sense of humour, Lord, and also things to laugh about. Give us the grace to take a joke against ourselves, and to see the funny side of the things we do. Save us from annoyance, bad temper, resentfulness against our friends. Help us to laugh even in the face of trouble. Fill our minds with the love of Jesus; for his name's sake.

A. G. Bullivant

For fine weather

Lord, Saint Benedict's sister prayed for rain and within an hour her prayer was heard. For the prophet Samuel and Elias thou didst do the same. Prayer then, can get the weather changed, and this is something which nothing else can do. And so I ask for the purely temporary favour of fine weather, knowing that thy providence will decide upon, what, taken all in all, is best.

Hubert van Zeller OSB

For acceptance of self

A little patience,
O God,

I am coming.
One must take nature as she is!
It was not I who made her!
I do not mean to criticize
this house on my back—
It has its points—
but you must admit, Lord,
it is heavy to carry!
Still,
let us hope that this double enclosure,
my shell and my heart,
will never be quite shut to You.

Prayer of the Tortoise,
Carmen Bernos de Gasztold

Dear God,
it is I, the elephant,
your creature,
who is talking to you.
I am so embarrassed by my great self,
and, truly, it is not my fault
if I spoil your jungle with my big feet.
Let me be careful and behave wisely,
always keeping my dignity and poise;
give me such philosophic thoughts
that I can rejoice everywhere I go
in the lovable oddity of things.

Prayer of the Elephant,
Carmen Bernos de Gasztold

For right use of time

    Lord,
help me to remember that all time belongs to you,
and that I am responsible to you for my use of it.
Help me neither to waste time
nor be so obsessed with saving it
that I become the slave of time
and lose my sense of proportion and values.
Lord,
teach me to use my time to your glory,
creatively,
re-creatively
in that rhythm of involvement in the world
and of withdrawal from the world
which is your will for me.
Save me both from running away from the world
into self-centred religiosity
and from running away from the inner life
into compulsive busyness.
Lord, help me to live each day
so that at the end of it
there is nothing I cannot share with you,
nothing for which I cannot thank you.

Margaret Dewey

    Dear God, give me time,
Men are always so driven!
Make them understand I can never hurry.
Give me time to eat;

Give me time to plod;
Give me time to sleep;
Give me time to think.

Prayer of the Ox,
Carmen Bernos de Gasztold

For friendship

O God, our heavenly Father, who hast commanded us to love one another as thy children, and has
ordained the highest friendship in the bond of thy
Spirit, we beseech thee to maintain and preserve us
always in the same bond, to thy glory, and our
mutual comfort, with all those to whom we are
bound by any special tie, either of nature or of
choice; that we may be perfected together in that
love which is from above, and which never faileth
when all other things shall fail.

Send down the dew of thy heavenly grace upon
us, that we may have joy in each other that passeth
not away; and having lived together in love here,
according to thy commandment, may live for ever
together with thee, being made one in thee, in thy
glorious kingdom hereafter, through Jesus Christ
our Lord.

George Hickes (1642-1715)

Discrimination

Lord, thou hast set us to live in this day and
generation.
We are summoned by books and magazines,

radio and television,
cinemas and the theatre.
Teach us to be discriminating and independent in
our use of these things.
Help us to recognise what is ostentatious, super-
ficial and insincere.
Give to men and women who are responsible for
modern advertising techniques
an understanding of what is essential and con-
structive.
Train public opinion to fulfil its critical function.
Give us parents, teachers and pastors
who will witness to you through their behaviour
and who will be real christian leaders
in the congregation, in management and in public
life.

Hans Storck

Posters

They are loud.
I cannot avoid them, for they crowd together on
the wall alluring and tempting,
their violent colours hurt my eyes
and I can't rid myself of their distasteful presence.
Lord, in the same way too often I draw attention
to myself.
Grant that I may be more humble and un-
obtrusive

and above all keep me from trying to impress through showy display,

For it is your light only, Lord, that must draw all men.

Michel Quoist

For help in race relations

I see white and black, Lord,
I see white teeth in a black face,
I see black eyes in a white face.
Help me to see *persons*, Jesus, not a black person,
or a white person, a red person or a yellow person,
but human persons.

Malcolm Boyd

When in love

O God,
thou who art love,
search our hearts.
Reveal to us in the way
that is best known to thee,
and in thine own good time,
whether we bear for each other
that pearl of thy bestowing,
human love.
Sanctify
our feelings towards each other.
Help us
to come before thee in prayerful silence
during this time of waiting.

O Father help us
to see thy will for us.
This we ask
in the name of our common Saviour
Jesus Christ.

Chandran Devanesen

IV

THANKSGIVING, JOY AND PRAISE

People who are not used to prayer think from outside that it is only for times of need, sickness or disaster. Yet, the more direct our realisation of God in our lives and in the world, the more we are filled with something we wish to pour out—a fulness of heart, rather than a constant stream of requests.

It may be necessary at first for you to train yourself to remember to thank, to recall God in your joy, to praise him for all that he is. What I mean is that when things are going fine, it is much easier to forget God than to thank him! But if we go out of our way to dig at ourselves over this when the time is there, it will gradually build up into a regular habit. Then it will be true as scripture says: Out of the fulness of the heart the mouth speaks. Then, automatically, the praise and joy and love of God will rest in and spring from our hearts as we explore God's part in our existence.

This kind of prayer and praise is linked so closely to all you are and all you feel that you may get flooded with the sense of God, his power, his majesty, your own littleness; you may thrill at his gentleness, gape at breadth and depth, be stilled by his love.

If this happens, do not be afraid. It may sound silly, but it is quite easy to be afraid. You may want to go into poetry, short prayers or ejaculations of love, speechless 'resting' in God, or a prolonged Alleluia.

Thanksgiving

Thanks be to thee, my Lord Jesus Christ, for all the benefits and blessings which thou hast given to me, for all the pains and insults which thou hast borne for me, O most merciful Friend, Brother and Redeemer; may I know thee more clearly, love thee more dearly, and follow thee more nearly.

Saint Richard of Chichester (died 1255)

I thank thee, Lord, for knowing me better than I know myself, and for letting me know myself better than others know me.

Make me, I pray, better than they suppose, and forgive me what they do not know.

Said to be by Abu Bekr (died 634), father-in-law of Muhammed

Most worthy art thou, O good and gracious God, of all praise, even for thine own sake which exceedeth all things in holiness. By thee only are we hallowed and made holy. As our duty continually bids us, we praise thee for our glorious redemption, purchased for us in thy dearly beloved Son, Jesus Christ. Give us, therefore, the Holy Spirit to govern us. And grant that all things that breathe with life may praise thee, through the same Jesus Christ, our Lord, who reigneth with thee and the Holy Ghost, one God for ever and ever.

The Iona Books

We thank thee, O Lord, for all who have chosen poverty or solitude for thy sake, for men of prayer, for saints in common life who have borne suffering for noble ends, and for those who have endured pain with patience and purity of life, in the strength of him who, for the joy that was set before him, endured the cross, even Jesus Christ our Lord.

Anonymous

We thank thee, O Father, for all those who hallow suffering; for those who in their thought for others leave no room for pity for themselves; for those whose faith brings light to the dark places of life; and for those whose patience inspires others to hold on. And grant, O loving Father, to all who are bound in the mysterious fellowship of suffering the sense of comradship with others and the knowledge of thy love, and give them thy peace which passes all understanding; through Jesus Christ our Lord.

Hugh L. Johnston

Modern thanksgiving

Look upon this universe, my Lord;
Remember it, for you created it out of love.
Look upon us and vindicate us.
And if I stand before you with all of mankind—
not because I am good but because you are good—
and offer this mankind to you,
I offer it in a sacrifice of thanksgiving.

We thank you, Lord.
We thank you for the bread we eat,
and for the people with whom we break that bread
and share.
We thank you for the streets and the buildings,
for the grass and the trees,
for the bridges and the automobiles,
and the farms and the ranches,
for the toll booths and the movie marquees
and the lakes and the fishes.
We thank you for the telephone company,
for the typewriters,
for the adding machines,
We thank you for the hay, new-mown,
for the corn which grows,
for the wheat, for the barley, for the vegetables.
We thank you for each other,
and we know full well that
half across the world
we are killing parts of ourselves.
Help us to learn, O Lord, that we are one.
We confess to you, my Lord, that we do not
realise what we are doing.
Lord forgive us. We do not understand.
We thank you for creation, for yourself.
As I have said, we do not know where we are going.
We are hardly sure of where we have been.
And as for the present, we are all confused,
But Lord, we believe. We do believe.
Help our unbelief.

Christopher William Jones

Glory be to God for dappled things—
For skies of couple-colour as a brinded cow;
For rose-moles all in stipple upon the trout that
swim;
Fresh-firecoal chestnut-falls; finches' wings;
Landscape plotted and pieced—fold, fallow and
plough;
And all trades, their gear and tackle and trim,
All things counter, original, spare and strange;
Whatever is fickle, freckled (who knows how?)
With swift, slow; sweet, sour; adazzle, dim;
He fathers-forth whose beauty is past change.
Praise him.

Gerard Manley Hopkins (1844-1889)

We give thee humble and hearty thanks, O most
merciful Father, for all thy goodness and loving-
kindness to us and to all men, for the blessings of
this life and for the promise of everlasting happiness. And as we are bound, we specially thank thee
for the mercies which we have received; for health
and strength, for outward prosperity and well-
being, for the many enjoyments of our daily life,
and the hope of the future; for the opportunities of
learning, for the knowledge of thy will, for the
means of serving thee in thy holy church, for the
love thou hast revealed to us in thy Son, our
Saviour; for every blessing of soul and body, we
thank thee, O God. Add this, O Lord, to thy other
mercies, that we may praise thee not with our lips

only, but with our lives, always looking to thee as the author and giver of all good things; for Jesus Christ's sake.

Brooke F. Westcott (1825-1901)

Praise to God

Glory be to God in the highest, and on earth peace, goodwill towards men; for unto us is born this day a Saviour who is Christ the Lord. We praise thee, we bless thee, we glorify thee, we give thanks to thee, for this greatest of thy mercies, O Lord God, heavenly King, God the Father almighty.

Bishop Thomas Ken (1637-1711)

You are holy, Lord, the only God,
    and your deeds are wonderful.
You are strong,
    You are great.
    You are the Most High,
    You are almighty.
    You, holy Father, are
    King of heaven and earth.
You are Three and One,
    Lord God, all good.
    You are good, all good, supreme good,
    Lord God, living and true.
You are love,
    You are wisdom.
    You are humility,

You are endurance.
You are rest,
You are peace.
You are joy and gladness,
You are justice and moderation.
You are all our riches,
And you suffice for us.
You are beauty,
You are gentleness.
You are our protector,
You are our guardian and defender.
You are courage,
You are our haven and our hope.
You are our faith,
Our great consolation.
You are our eternal life,
Great and wonderful Lord,
God almighty,
Merciful Saviour.

Saint Francis of Assisi (1182-1226)

The heavens shall praise thy wonders;
But more the powers of my immortal soul,
Which thou hast made more excellent than the
clouds, and greater than the Heavens!
O Lord, I rejoice and am exceeding glad;
Because of thy goodness,
In creating the world.
But much more abundantly,
For the glory of my soul;
Which cut out of nothing thou hast builded
To be a temple unto God,

A living temple of thine omnipresence,
  An understanding eye,
  A temple of eternity,
  A temple of thy wisdom, blessedness, and glory.
O ye powers of mine immortal Soul, bless ye the
  Lord, praise him and magnify him for ever.
  He hath made you greater,
  More glorious, brighter,
  Better than the heavens,
A meeter dwelling place for his eternal Godhead
  Than the heaven of heavens.
  The heaven of heavens,
  And all the spaces above the heavens,
  Are not able to contain him.
Being but dead and silent place,
  They feel not themselves.
  They know nothing,
  See no immensity nor wideness at all.
But in thee, my soul, there is a perceptive power
To measure all spaces beyond the heavens
And those spaces
  By him into thee
To feel and see the heaven of heavens
  All things contained in them,
  And his presence in thee.
Nor canst thou only feel his omnipresence in thee,
  But adore his goodness,
  Dread his power,
  Reverence his majesty,
  See his wisdom,
  Rejoice in his bounty,
  Conceive his eternity,

Praise his glory.
Which being things transcendent unto place,
Cannot by the heavens at all be apprehended.
　With reverence, O God, and dread mixed with joy, I come before thee.
　To consider thy glory in the perfection of my soul
The workmanship of the Lord.

Thomas Traherne (c 1636-1674)

Holy, holy, holy Lord God almighty!
Early in the morning our song shall rise to thee;
Holy, holy, holy, merciful and mighty,
God in three persons, blessed Trinity!
Holy, holy, holy, though the darkness hide thee,
Though the eye of sinful man thy glory may not see,
Only thou art holy; there is none beside thee,
Perfect in power, in love and purity.

Reginald Heber (1783-1826)

　I will magnify thee, O God, my King, and I will praise thy name for ever and ever.
　Every day will I give thanks unto thee, and praise thy name for ever and ever.
　Great is the Lord, and marvellous worthy to be praised; there is no end of his greatness.
　The Lord is gracious, and merciful, long-suffering and of great goodness.
　The Lord is loving unto every man, and his mercy is over all his works.
　All thy works praise thee, O Lord: and thy saints give thanks unto thee.

The Lord upholdeth all such as fall: and lifteth up all those that are down.

The Lord is nigh unto all them that call upon him: yea, all such as call upon him faithfully.

He will fulfil the desire of them that fear him: he also will hear their cry and will help them.

The Lord preserveth all them that love him: but scattereth abroad all the ungodly.

My mouth shall speak the praise of the Lord: and let all flesh give thanks unto his holy name for ever and ever.

Psalm 145 (Book of Common Prayer)

Praise be to him who when I call on him answers me, slow though I am when he calls me.

Praise be to him who gives to me when I ask him, miserly though I am when he asks a loan of me.

Praise be to him to whom I confide my needs whensoever I will and he satisfies them.

My Lord I praise thee, for thou art of my praise most worthy.

Muslim prayer

Blessed art thou, O Lord, the God of Israel our Father, for ever and ever. Thine, O Lord, is the greatness, and the power and the glory, and the victory, and the majesty; for all that is in the heavens and in the earth is thine; thine is the kingdom, O Lord, and thou art exalted as head above all. Both riches and honour come of thee,

and thou rulest over all. In thine hand are power
and might; and in thine hand it is to make great and
to give strength to all. And now we thank thee, our
God, and praise thy glorious name.

I Chronicles 29, 10-13

Lord, be it thine,
Unfaltering praise of mine!
To thee my whole heart's love be given,
Of earth and heaven thou king divine.
Lord, be it thine,
Unfaltering praise of mine!
And, O pure prince, make clear my way
To serve and pray at thy sole shrine!
Lord, be it thine,
Unfaltering praise of mine!
O father of all souls that long,
Take my song and make it thine.

Translated from the Irish by Robin Flower

V

INTERCESSION

Though we are selfish, there can be very few who do not have a desire at some time or other—perhaps very often indeed—to pray or intercede for someone else or for some cause.

There are many examples of this type of prayer, because this seems to be basic to our nature. The main point to make is that the virtue of these prayers is not the language used but your own sincere and convinced approach to God as the creator who loves you and cares for his creation, and who is not a fierce, distant, despotic monarch, but a friend and brother—one who listens and listens effectively.

When you are out of touch with someone you love, when vast miles separate you, when physical or mental distress tears you apart, when you are alone and anxious, when you desperately want something you are doing to succeed, when a loved one is dying and you can only sit at the bedside— there is intercession, there is God to turn to.

Learn to rely on intercession, keeping your pleas, however desperate, within the limits of God's will, though freely expressing the fulness of your own desire.

In the development of prayer, you should grow more aware of what redemption means, since as you come to know God more deeply and sense his presence within you, you should become more conscious of being used by him in the redemption of the world. As this happens, you will discover the needs of individuals, friends, neighbours, the neighbourhood, flooding in, along with the conscious urge to make yourself a sacrifice or intercession. It is not simply that you want to go on asking, but also somehow the gift of yourself will become part of the intercession, and in some way you will sense that you are sharing the burden of others.

FOR ALL SORTS AND CONDITIONS OF MEN

For all sorts and conditions of men

O God, the creator and preserver of all mankind, we humbly beseech thee for all sorts and conditions of men; that thou wouldst be pleased to make thy ways known to them, thy saving health to all the nations. More especially we pray for the good estate of the Catholic church; that it may be so guided and governed by thy good Spirit, that all who profess and call themselves Christians may be led in the way of truth, and hold the faith in unity of spirit, in the bond of peace, and in righteousness of life. Finally we commend to thy fatherly goodness all those who are in any way afflicted or distressed in mind, body or estate, that it may please thee to comfort and relieve them according to their several necessities, giving them patience under their sufferings, and a happy issue out of all their afflictions. And this we beg for Jesus Christ, his sake.

Book of Common Prayer

The work of prayer

My God and Father,
help me to pray
as my first work,
mine unremitting work,

my highest, finest, and dearest work;
as the work I do for thee, and by thee,
and with thee,
for thy other children and for the whole world.
Infuse and influence it with thy blessed Spirit,
that it be not unwilling, nor unworthy, nor in vain;
that it be not occupied with my own concerns,
nor dwell in the interests dear to myself;
but seek thy purposes, thy glory only;
that it be holy and more holy to the Holiest,
and ever and all through thy Son,
my Saviour Jesus Christ.

Eric Milner-White

The work of intercession

The passer-by from Cyrene

Was he afraid, Lord?
I expect so,
The soldiers bearing down on him, giving him no
  choice, forcing him to carry the cross, that
  heavy cross.
Would they execute him too?
Was there fear in his heart as he walked along
  with Jesus to the place of the scull?
To get involved in another man's problems
  carries risks and anxieties with it.
Can I really help?
Can I listen?
Can I suffer along with the sufferer?

Do I have to feel, Lord, that I must be able to
   provide a pat answer,
a text-book solution?
Like the man from Cyrene perhaps, my own
   security and comfort is at the front of my mind.
Support me, Lord, so I may support that man
   over there who has his cross to bear.

Rex Chapman

Make us worthy, Lord, to serve our fellow men
throughout the world who live and die in poverty
and hunger. Give them through our hands this day
their daily bread, and by our understanding love,
give peace and joy.

Mother Teresa of Calcutta

For ourselves

   Loving and Holy Spirit of God we pray:
   That we and all men may increasingly work
together to establish the kingdom of God on earth;
   That the resources of the world may be gathered,
distributed and used with unselfish motives and
scientific skill for the greatest benefit for all;
   That beauty may be given to our towns, and left
to our countryside;
   That children may be finely bred and finely
trained;
   That there may be open ways, and peace, and
freedom from end to end of the earth;
   And that all men may learn to be lovers through
keeping thy company. In the name of Jesus.

G. C. Binyon

For all mankind

We pray for all mankind,
Though divided into nations and races,
Yet are all men thy children,
Drawing from thee their life and being,
Commanded by thee to obey thy laws,
Each in accordance with the power to know and
    understand them.
Cause hatred and strife to vanish,
That abiding peace may fill the earth,
And humanity may everywhere be blessed with the
    fruit of peace.
So shall the spirit of brotherhood among men,
Show forth their faith that
Thou art the Father of all.
Jewish prayer from the Liberal Jewish Prayer Book

For forgiveness of all mankind

O Lord, forgive the cruelties of men of every age,
    their insensibility to other's pain,
    the deliberation that gives pain to satisfy and
express the evil that rebels from love's surrender to
other's needs to exalt itself.
    O Lord, forgive the carelessness that passes by
the blunted conscience that will not see or fear to see,
    the wrongs men do to other men.
    Most merciful, most loving Judge, Redeemer of
mankind,
    Thou dost restore the fallen,
    Thou dost seek out the scattered sheep.

Gilbert Shaw

For peace in the world

Almighty God, from whom all thoughts of truth and peace proceed, kindle, we pray thee, in the hearts of all men the true love of peace; and guide with thy pure and peaceable wisdom those who take counsel for the nations of the earth; that in tranquillity thy kingdom may go forward, till the earth be filled with the knowledge of thy love: through Jesus Christ our Lord.

Francis Paget (1851-1911)

For disarmament

Lord, here is your cross,
   You must bear it alone.
It is too hard for us,
   We need other defences.
It is too simple,
   We must have our strategists.
We know all the arguments,
   We have never heard yours.
Lord, argue with us,
   Show us new ways,
Get us out of this situation
   We landed ourselves in,
For your world's sake.

A prayer used at the launching of the Polaris submarine, February 1967

For fellow-workers

O God, who hast bound us together in this bundle of life, give us grace to understand how our lives depend on the courage, the industry, the honesty, and integrity of our fellow men; that we may be mindful of their needs, grateful for their faithfulness, and faithful in our responsibilities to them; through Jesus Christ our Lord.

Reinhold Niebuhr

For workers

O God, the creator of all things, who hast made man in thine own image, so that he must ever seek his joy in creative work, have mercy, we beseech thee, on all who are unemployed, or whose work is dull; and help us so to order our common life that every man may have work to do and find joy in doing it, to the good of all mankind and to the glory of thy name, through Jesus Christ our Lord.

New Every Morning

Race relations

Grant us, O Lord, to see in our coloured countrymen, our nearest neighbours to love as ourselves, equally with us the brothers and sisters for whom Christ died. Give us grace to welcome them into our national life, to help them to find a satisfactory place in it, and to receive from them gifts which we may have lost. Save us from racial pride, colour prejudice, personal indifference, and desire for apartness. And grant that we may all become a new race in Christ Jesus, the Lord and Saviour of all.

George Appleton

For a friend

I pray thee, good Lord Jesus, by the love thou hadst for thy young disciple John, to make me thankful for all thou hast given me in my friend. Bless him exceedingly above all that I can ask or think. Help us to be one in heart through all separations, and walk together in the path of thy service, and finally unite us in the place where love is perfect and immortal, even with thyself.

William Bright (1824-1901)

For the old

Eternal God, who through the passing years remain ever the same, be near to all who are aged or infirm. Though their bodies fail let their spirits be strong in thee, that with patience they may bear weariness and distress, and at the last may meet death unafraid, through Jesus Christ our Lord.

New Every Morning

Let us pray for the elderly and the old that they will remain young in spirit. Keep them from being unthinkingly critical of young people whose ways are not their ways. Give them understanding of the present-day world, of the ideals and ideas of teen-agers many of whom hate war and fear and despise the establishment. Help the old not to fear change nor to cling to institutions which have ceased to have meaning for other generations. Let us pray that the old may be able, out of their experience, to help young people in an understanding and uncondescending way. And teach us all, O Lord, how to learn from each other and to find you in everyone we encounter.

Etta Gullick

For children

O Lord Jesus, be near to all young children, that in the peril and confusion of this age their growing spirits may take no hurt at our hands, and grant to parents such sure knowledge of thy love that they may guide their children with courage and faith.

New Every Morning

For our homes

O Jesus Christ, our brother, our Lord: you lived in a home at Nazareth; you obeyed your parents, worked with your father, and enjoyed the company of your friends and relations. Think of our homes now, and bless them for us. Strengthen the love that we have for one another; give all that we need for our welfare and happiness. In a word, Lord, make our homes like your home; for your name's sake.

Christopher Campling

FOR THE CHURCH AND FOR UNITY

The Church

O most gracious Father, we most humbly beseech thee for thy holy Catholic church. Fill it with all truth; in all truth with all peace. Where it is corrupt, purge it; where it is in error, direct it; where anything is amiss, reform it; where it is right, strengthen and confirm it; where it is in want, furnish it; where it is divided, heal it and unite it in thy love; through Jesus Christ our Lord.

William Laud (1573-1645)

For unity and strength

O thou God of peace, unite our hearts by thy bond of peace, that we may live with one another continually in gentleness and humility, in peace and unity. O thou God of patience, give us patience in time of trial and steadfastness to endure to the end. O thou Spirit of prayer, awaken our hearts, that we may lift up holy hands to God, and cry unto him in all our distresses. Be our defence and shade in time of need, our help in trial, our consolation when all things are against us. Come, O thou eternal light, salvation and comfort, be our light in darkness, salvation in life, our comfort in death, and lead us in the strait way to everlasting life, that we may praise thee for ever, through Jesus Christ, our Lord.

Bernard Albrecht (d. 1636)

For unity among Christians

O God the Father, Origin of Divinity, Good that is beyond all that is good, Fair beyond all that is fair, in whom is calmness, peace and concord; do thou make up the dissensions which divide us from each other, and bring us back to a unity of love, which may bear some likeness to thy divine nature. And as thou art above all things, make us one by the unanimity of a good mind, that through the embrace of charity and the bonds of affection, we may be spiritually one, as well in ourselves as in each other; through that peace of thine which maketh all things peaceful, and through the grace, the mercy, and tenderness of thy Son, Jesus Christ.

Saint Dionysius, Patriarch of the
Syrian Jacobite Church (b. 818)

O Lord God, the one God, make thy people one. Whatever our differences, even in matters essential, may we ever realise that we are one in Christ Jesus. Let not Satan break the blessed bond of union between believers, but may it be increasingly strengthened in our own experience, and in all thy people everywhere, for the sake of Jesus Christ our Redeemer.

Benjamin Jenks (1647-1724)

Lord Jesus Christ
who hast made peace by the blood
of thy Cross

and now
ever livest to make intercession for us
ever praying that we may be one
as thou art one with the Father
in the love of the Holy Spirit
bring all those who have been
baptized into thee
bring all those who love thee
in sincerity
bring all men
into one body
at the last
Amen.

E. S. Abbott

FOR THOSE IN NEED, DISTRESS OR SUFFERING

Prayers of petition

We pray to you
for all who are crucified
like your Son,
for all who are forsaken by you,
for all who cannot endure their fate,
for all who suffer
and cannot see why.
For all who are rebellious
or exhausted and stunned,
for those who are bitter and cynical,
turned in on themselves
and scornful of others—
make them mild and open their eyes again
to the goodness that is possible among men
and to your creation and to your future.
For all who are viewed with mistrust,
who live under the pressure
of suspicion and evil gossip,
for all whose self-confidence has been undermined
by the harsh criticism of others,
for all who are misunderstood
and who never hear a kind word
or meet anyone who will accept them.
For all who are anxious or inhibited,
for those whose consciences are warped and not free,
for all who are tense and restless,

uncertain or at their wit's end.
For all who are the victims
of blackmail or corruption,
for all whose lives are wrecked
by their involvement with the gods
and powers of darkness—
that they may, in their defencelessness,
resemble your Son Jesus
who was defenceless
in the hands of men.
For all who have to live with injustice,
who are caught up in an inhuman system
and who cannot make any headway under it.
For all soldiers at the front
who have to fight and kill
against their will and against their consciences.
For all those who want war
and whose aim is to divide men.
For those who make money
from the destruction of others.
For all those whose minds are poisoned and
    dangerous—
that they may be freed from their inhumanity
and granted forgiveness.
For all who have lost heart
Because of so much evil in the world.
but also for those who are optimistic,
for all those who radiate strength
and can offer friendship—
that they may not fail when they are tested
and that we may never lack their companionship.
We pray to you

for all who have no form of beauty
to look up to,
for those who cannot keep up with others,
for children who have been born unlucky,
for all those who are disturbed or handicapped,
for all those who are incurably ill.
We ask you
that we may discover the meaning
of their presence in this world.

Huub Oosterhuis

General intercession for those in trouble

O God the Father, bless those for whom life is very
    difficult,
those who have difficult decisions to make, and
    who honestly do not know what is the right thing
    to do;
those who have difficult tasks to do and to face, and
    who fear they may fail in them;
those who have difficult temptations to face, and
    who know only too well that they may fall to
    them, if they try to meet them alone;
those who have a difficult temperament and nature
    to master, and who know that they can be their
    own worst enemies;
those who have difficult people to work with, those
    who have to suffer unjust treatment, unfair
    criticism, unappreciated work;
those who are sad because someone they loved has
    died;

those who are disappointed in something for which
   they hoped very much;
those who have been hurt by their enemies, or,
   what is far more bitter, by the faithlessness and
   the disloyalty of their friends.
Bless us, O God, with whatever we need and we are
   bringing to you now.

William Barclay

For those in distress

Lord Jesus, when you were on earth, they brought
the sick to you and you healed them all. Today we
ask you to bless all those in sickness, in weakness
and in pain:
   those who are blind and who cannot see the light
   of the sun, the beauty of the world, or the faces
   of their friends;
   those who are deaf and cannot hear the voices
   which speak to them;
   those who are helpless and who must lie in bed
   while others go out and in:
   Bless all such.
   those whose minds have lost their reason;
   those who are so nervous that they cannot cope
   with life;
   those who worry about everything:
   Bless all such.
   those who must face life under some handicap;
   those whose weakness means that they must
   always be careful;

those who are lame and maimed and cannot enter into any of the strenuous activities or pleasures of life;
those who have been crippled by accident, or by illness, or who were born with a weakness of body or mind:
Bless all such.
Grant that we in our health and our strength may never find those who are weak and handicapped a nuisance, but grant that we may always do and give all that we can to help them and to make life easier for them.

William Barclay

I am thinking tonight, Lord, of all the isolated ones:
Of all those who are alone, utterly alone,
Because they have never let go and be carried by any one,
Because they have never given themselves to you, Lord;
Those who know something that others will never know;
Those who suffer from a sore that no one can ever tend;
Those who are bled from a wound that no one will ever heal;
Those who are scared by a vicious blow that no one will ever suspect;
Those who locked in the terrifying silence of their hearts, a harvest of humiliation, despairs, hatreds;

Those who have hidden a mortal sin—cold sepulchres behind cheerful fronts.

The solitude of man frightens me, Lord;

Every man is alone, since he is unique;

And that solitude is sacred; he alone can break through it, confide and share confidences.

He alone can pass from solitude to communion.

And you want this communion, Lord, you want us to be united with one another;

In spite of the gulf that we have dug between us by sin you want us to be united as your Father and you are united.

Lord that boy hurts me, as do all isolated ones,

Grant that I may love them enough to break through their isolation.

Grant that I may pass through the world with all doors open,

My house entirely empty, available, welcoming.

Help me to withdraw so as to embarrass no one,

That others may come in without asking,

That they may deposit their burdens without being seen.

And I'll come, silently, to get them by night,

And you, Lord, will help me to bear them.

Michel Quoist

For those affected by sudden calamity

O God, I remember before you those on whom at this time disaster has come:

Bless those whose dear ones have been killed, and those whose dear ones lost their lives in seeking to save the lives of others.

Bless those who have lost their homes, those who
have seen all that they toiled for for a lifetime to
build up lost in an hour.

Help us always to remember those whose job it is to
risk their lives to rescue others or to keep them
safe—those in the fire service, in the police service,
in the medical service.

We shall forget this disaster, but we ask you always
to remember those who will never forget, because
life for them can never again be the same.

This we ask for your love's sake.

William Barclay

For prisoners

Lord Jesus Christ,
thou wast poor
and in distress, a captive and forsaken as I am.
Thou knowest all men's troubles;
Thou abidest with me
when all men fail me;
Thou rememberest and seekest me;
It is thy will that I should know thee
and turn to thee.
Lord, I hear thy call and follow;
Do thou help me.
O Holy Spirit,
give me faith that will protect me
from despair, from passions, and from vice;
Give me such love for God and men
as will blot out all hatred and bitterness;
Give me the hope that will deliver me

from fear and faint-heartedness.
O holy and merciful God,
my Creator and Redeemer,
my Judge and Saviour,
thou knowest me and all that I do.
Thou dost hate and punish evil without respect of
persons
in this world and the next;
Thou forgivest the sins of those
who sincerely pray for forgiveness;
Thou lovest goodness, and rewardest it on this earth
with a clear conscience,
and, in the world to come,
with a crown of righteousness.
I remember in thy presence all my loved ones,
my fellow-prisoners, and all who in this house
perform their hard service;
Lord, have mercy.
Restore me to liberty
and enable me to so live now
that I may answer before thee and before men.
Lord, whatever this day may bring,
thy name be praised.
Amen.

Dietrich Bonhoeffer (1906-1945)

For the sick, the hungry, the lonely

Lord, comfort the sick, the hungry, the lonely and
those who are hurt and shut in on themselves, by
your presence in their hearts; use us to help them
in a practical way. Show us how to set about this

and give us strength, tact and compassion. Teach us how to be alongside them, and how to share in their distress in the depth of our being and in our prayer. Make us open to them and give us courage to suffer with them, and that in so doing we share with you in the suffering of the world for we are your body on earth and you work through us.

Etta Gullick

Prayer for the hungry of the World*
O Lord,
our meal is steaming before us
and it smells very good.
The water is clear and fresh.
We are happy and satisfied.
But now we must think of our sisters
and brothers all over the world
who have nothing to eat
and only a little to drink.
Please, please, let them have enough to eat
and enough to drink.
That is most important.
But give them also
what they need every day
in order to get through in this life.
Just as you have given enough to eat and drink
to the people of Israel in the desert
please give it also to our hungry and thirsty
   brothers,
now and at anytime.

An African Christian

---

* *Can be also used as a grace before meals.*

For the homeless

Have mercy, O Lord our God, on those whom war or oppression or famine have robbed of homes and friends, and aid all those who try to help them. We commend also into thy care those whose homes are broken by conflict and lack of love; grant that where the love of man has failed, the divine compassion may heal; through Jesus Christ our Lord.

'New Every Morning'

For the homeless or badly housed

O God, who wouldst not that any should live without comfort and hope, have compassion on the multitudes in our day who have no homes, or who are overcrowded in wretched dwellings. Bless and inspire those who are labouring for their good. Stir the conscience of the whole nation, O Lord, and both break the bonds of covetousness and make plain the way of deliverance for the sake of Jesus Christ, our Saviour.

Frank Colquhoun

For the lonely

O God of love, who art in all places and times, pour thy spirit of healing and comfort upon every lonely heart. Have pity upon those who are bereft of human love, and on those to whom it has never

come. Be unto them a strong consolation, and in
the end give them the fulness of joy; for the sake of
Jesus Christ our Lord.

Anonymous

Almighty God, look upon those who are lonely
and hungry-hearted, the uncompanioned, the un-
wanted: on whom all who feel themselves left out
and in exile from the joys for which they long.
Grant them, O God, some comradeship of understanding and affection, arouse in them an interest or
engage them in activity to comfort them in discon-
tent or desolation; and if at times they see that there
is no one who would know them, be thou a place
for them to flee to, and cheer them with the welcome
of thy love; through Jesus Christ our Lord.

Miles Lowell Yates

For drug takers

Lord, we lay before you those who are enslaved
by drugs and those who are attracted by them. We
are to blame for their plight; we have accepted the
material civilization of our age, and have not
proclaimed your life-giving gospel with all its glory
and mystery. We are responsible for the loneliness
and frustration which made them turn to drugs.
Lord, give addicts strength to leave their drugs and
turn to you, and show us how to help them. Make
us sympathetic and understanding of them so that

we too may be able to share their burdens which are both yours and ours through your Son who bore the sins of the world on the cross and who rose again in glory and mystery.

Etta Gullick

For incurables

O heavenly Father, we pray thee for those suffering from diseases for which at present there is no cure. Give them the victory of trust and hope, that they may never lose their faith in thy loving purpose. Grant thy wisdom to all who are working to discover the secrets of disease, and the faith that through thee all things are possible. We ask this in the name of him who went about doing good and healing all kinds of diseases, even thy Son, Jesus Christ our Lord.

George Appleton

For the despondent

Comfort we beseech thee, most gracious God, all who are cast down and faint of heart amidst the sorrows and difficulties of the world; grant that by the energy of thy Holy Spirit they may be enabled to go upon their way rejoicing and give thee continual thanks for thy sustaining providence; through Jesus Christ, our Saviour.

Richard Meux Benson (1824-1913)

Almighty God, look down upon those who are weighed down by uncongenial or exhausting tasks or by crippling responsibilities; whose lot is disappointment and frustration, whose freedoms are enchained, whose hopes are forfeit.

Strengthen them, O God, for burden-bearing; give them a gallant spirit for performing all hard duties as necessity demands; let their load be sometimes lightened by being shared, if it may not be removed; and refresh them in their heaviness as thou alone canst do, through Jesus Christ our Lord.

Miles Lowell Yates

For the handicapped

O loving Father, we pray for all who are handicapped in the race of life; the blind, the defective and the delicate, and all who are permanently injured. We pray for those worn out with sickness and those who are wasted with misery, for the dying and all unhappy children. May they learn the mystery of the road of suffering which Christ has trodden and the saints have followed, and bring thee this gift that angels cannot bring, a heart that trusts thee even in the dark; and this we ask in the name of him who himself took our infirmities upon him, even the same Jesus Christ, our Saviour.

A. S. T. Fisher

For our sick friend or relation

O merciful Lord of life and health, look we beseech thee, upon our loved one who is sick. Renew his/her strength, and restore him/her to health, if it be thy gracious will. Give him/her in the time of bodily weakness the renewal of thy Spirit and the upholding power of thy love; and as all things work together for good to them that love thee, so do thou shed abroad in his/her heart thy love, that out of this weakness, he/she may grow stronger in thee and thy grace, through Jesus Christ our Lord.

'Prayers for Family Worship'

Lord, the one that I love is sick and in great pain; out of your compassion heal him and take away his pain. It breaks my heart to see him suffer; may I not share his pain if it is not your will that he be healed? Lord, let him know that you are with him; support and help him that he may come to know you more deeply as a result of his suffering. Lord be our strength and support in this time of darkness and give us that deep peace which comes from trusting you.

Etta Gullick

For the sick

We earnestly beseech you, our Redeemer, to bring to this thy servant the grace of the Holy Ghost as a healing remedy, for all his ills. Bind up his wounds; forgive his sins; rid him of all anguish

of mind and body. Restore, in thy mercy, full health
to his body and soul, so that with thy help he may
be well again and able to take up his work and
duties of life again.

'The Small Ritual'

Holy Lord and Father, almighty and eternal God,
who dost pour into broken human bodies the healing grace of thy own blessing and in a thousand
ways dost show thy care for what thy hands have
made, be good to us and draw near, as we call
upon thy name. Deliver thy servant from his sickness. Give him health anew. Stretch out thy hand
and set him on his feet again. Put strength into him
and keep him safe under thy powerful protection.
Give him back again to thy holy church, and may
all henceforth be well with him. Through Christ
our Lord.

'The Small Ritual'

That suffering may be creative

Lord we pray thee for all who are weighed down
with the mystery of suffering. Reveal thyself to
them as the God of love who thyself dost bear all
our sufferings. Grant that they may know that
suffering borne in fellowship with thee is not waste
or frustration, but can be turned to goodness and
blessing, something greater than if they had never
suffered, through him who on the cross suffered
rejection and hatred, loneliness and despair,

agonizing pain and physical death, and rose victorious from the dead, conquering and to conquer, even Jesus Christ, our Lord.

George Appleton

The dying

O Lord Jesus Christ, who in thy last agony didst commend thy spirit into the hands of thy heavenly Father: have mercy upon all sick and dying persons; may death be unto them the gate of ever-lasting life; and give them the assurance of thy presence even in the dark valley; for thy name's sake who art the resurrection and the life, and to whom be glory for ever and ever.

Adapted from the Sarum Primer

For the dead

Remember, O Lord, the souls of thy servants, who have gone before us with the sign of faith, and slumber and sleep in peace. We beseech thee, O Lord, graciously to grant to them and all who rest in Christ a place of refreshment, light, and peace; through the same Christ our Lord.

The Roman Canon

May the souls of the faithful departed, through the mercy of God, rest in peace.

For those who mourn

O Lord,
who healest the broken-hearted
and bindest up their wounds,
grant thy consolation unto mourners.
O strengthen and support them
in their day of grief and sorrow;
and remember them (and their children)
for a long and good life.
Put into their hearts the fear and love of thee;
that they may serve thee with a perfect heart
and let their latter end be peace.

From the Jewish 'Authorized Daily Prayer Book'

O God, please be very close to all those who are
mourning for the loss of someone they loved. May
you be their comfort and their strength; through
Jesus Christ our Lord.

Beryl Bye

VI

THE SPIRIT WHO WORKS

We are told in the scriptures of the work of the Spirit in us. So it is not unnatural that you may at times feel conscious of the Spirit, or at least a desire for his presence and working in you.

As you go on, prayer may be difficult; you may not know where to turn or what to say. It is a funny phrase to say 'be open to the Spirit', but in fact it does mean something, it combines emptiness and yearning and muddle and so on. It is Saint Paul saying that the Spirit 'groans in me awaiting the adoption of the sons of God'; or as he also says 'the Spirit will speak for you, when you do not know what to say'. This very simple acceptance of the Spirit means that you can sense the Spirit using your mood or state, even when you can feel nothing except aridity and boredom (if you can accept that paradox).

In essence, this is the Spirit who is Love. It is obvious then that his fundamental effect is to transform us in love. You cannot open yourself to the Spirit truly and remain cold, hard, unkind and so on.

It is worth looking again at Saint Paul . . . He speaks of charity . . . love. He says it is 'patient', 'kind' and so on. These attributes should be mirrored in our development, especially in our patience in prayer and in living with others. We are also told that the fruits of the Spirit are 'love, joy, peace, patience'.

If you can realise yourself as the temple of the Holy Spirit, joy will often well up from inside you and need to be expressed by you; peace will invade and envelop you, a deep peace. This does not mean that all troubles pass away; there will be the usual petty trials and turmoils; there will be the usual physical pains and mental griefs; indeed, they will be intensified. But deep, deep down there will be an unshakable, undisturbed, relaxed, calm bed of peace. This is 'the peace the world cannot give'. Once you have experienced this and know what it is about, you will say: 'Yes, I know what you mean'; if you have not yet entered this experience, I can only say: 'Open yourself to the Spirit and long for the peace of Christ with all your heart'.

One way or another, it is vital to your prayer life, and your whole life in relation to God and the community that you should be filled with the Spirit of God.

The Holy Spirit

Come thou, Holy Spirit;
restore the lives which, without thee, are dead;
kindle the hearts which, without thee, are cold and
dull;
enlighten the minds which, without thee, are dark
and blind;
fill the Church which, without thee, is an empty
shrine, and teach us to pray.

'New Every Morning'

O Spirit of God
    who dost speak to spirits
    created in thine own likeness;
penetrate into the depths of our spirits,
    into the storehouse of memories,
    remembered and forgotten,
    into the depths of being,
    the very springs of personality.
    and cleanse and forgive,
    making us whole and holy,
    that we may be thine
    and live in the new being
    of Christ our Lord.

George Appleton

Holy Spirit, Lord of light,
    From the clear celestial height
    Thy pure beaming radiance give.

Come, thou Father of the poor,
   Come with treasures which endure,
   Come thou light of all that live!
Thou of all consolers best.
   Thou the soul's delightful guest,
   Dost refreshing peace bestow.
Thou in toil art comfort sweet,
   Pleasant coolness in the heat,
   Solace in the midst of woe.
Light immortal, light divine,
   Visit thou these hearts of thine,
   And our inmost being fill.
If thou take thy grace away
   Nothing pure in man will stay;
   All his good is turned to ill.
Heal our wounds, our strength renew.
   On our dryness pour thy dew,
   Wash the stains of guilt away.
Bend the stubborn heart and will;
   Melt the frozen, warm the chill;
   Guide the steps that go astray.
Thou on us, who ever more
   Thee confess and thee adore,
   With thy sevenfold gifts descend:
Give us comfort when we die,
   Give us life with thee on high;
   Give us joys that never end.

Attributed to
Archbishop Langton (1150-1228)

In the hour of my distress,
When temptations me oppress,

And when I my sins confess,
Sweet Spirit comfort me!
When I lie within my bed,
Sick in heart, and sick in head,
And with doubts discomforted,
Sweet spirit comfort me!
When the house doth sigh and weep,
And the world is drawn in sleep,
Yet mine eyes the watch do keep;
Sweet Spirit comfort me!
When (God knows) I'm tossed about,
Either with despair or doubt;
Yet before the glass be out,
Sweet Spirit comfort me!
When the judgment is reveal'd
And that open'd that was seal'd,
When to thee I have appeal'd
Sweet Spirit comfort me!

Robert Herrick (1591-1674)

O God the Holy Ghost who art Light
   unto thine elect,
      evermore enlighten us.
Thou who art Fire of Love,
   evermore enkindle us.
Thou who art Lord and Giver of Life,
   evermore live in us.
Thou who bestowest sevenfold grace,
   evermore replenish us.
As the wind is thy symbol,
   so forward our goings.

As the dove,
   so launch us heavenwards;
As water,
   so purify our spirits;
As a cloud,
   so abate our temptations;
As dew,
   so revive our languor;
As fire,
   so purge our dross.

Christina Rossetti (1830-1894)

Most Holy Spirit, Comforter Divine,
   through thee the life of prayer is made complete,
   through thee the suffering pilgrimage is made
      joyful,
   through thee the darkness is made light:
illumine thou my life, inspire my prayer,
be thou the unity that makes me one,
that I may be all prayer,
one coinherence with my Source and End,
one coinherence with the world of men and nature's
      order,
   one wholeness in myself;
   purged, restored, reunited in the life
   from which man fell
   and which the passion of the Lord restored
   a temple for thy majesty.

Gilbert Shaw

Look graciously upon us, O Holy Spirit, and give us, for our hallowing, thoughts which pass into prayer, prayers which pass into love, and love which passes into life with thee for ever.

'New Every Morning'

Love

O Lord, who hast taught us that all our doings without love are nothing worth, send thy Holy Ghost, and pour into our hearts that most excellent gift of love, the very bond of peace and all virtues, without which whosoever liveth is counted dead before thee; grant us this for thy only Son Jesus Christ's sake.

'Book of Common Prayer'
Thomas Cranmer (1489-1556)

Almighty and eternal God, who hast revealed thy nature in Christ Jesus thy son as love, we humbly pray thee give us thy Holy Spirit to glorify thee also in our hearts as pure love, and thus constrain us by thy divine power to love thee with our whole souls, and our brethren as ourselves; that so by thy grace we may be fulfilled with love, and evermore abide in thee, and thou in us, with all joyfulness, and free from fear or distrust; through Jesus Christ our Lord.

Christian C. J. Bunsen (1791-1860)

Let the fire of thy love, O God, cleanse and possess our souls; that out of pure hearts and true affections we may worship thee; through Jesus Christ our Lord.

'New Every Morning'

Lord Jesus, you have taught us that love is the fulfilling of the law. Teach us now what love really is, how much it costs, how far it leads, how deep it digs into our selfish selves. Then give us the courage and the generosity to accept what this means today and tomorrow and in the whole future way of our lives.

Michael Hollings

O thou, who hast so loved my soul, make me a lover of souls. Fill me with an unwearied, unpossessive love, of keen perception and strong fibre, that shall help others to do their best. Help me to be an advocate of the absent, and cast out from me the dumb spirit of nervousness or self-absorption, which hinders me from showing the love I feel. Heal my heart of all uncontrolled affection, that being cured and thoroughly cleansed, I may be made fit to love, steady to persevere. Let no sickness or cross accident, no employment or weariness make me ungracious to those about me, but in all things make me like unto thy holy Jesus.

Anonymous

O Lord God, make my religion to be my love, my deepest love, my delight, the love of my life.

Let me never be content with giving thee less than my whole heart; and that, with no motive which is not pure, no mind which is not joyful.

Make all my days a looking up and a going forth to greet and meet that majesty of love which has visited and redeemed thy people:—the love that would save to the uttermost and is the glory of thy glory, illimitable, inexhaustible, world without end.

Eric Milner-White

O God, the God of all goodness and of all grace, who art worthy of a greater love than we can either give or understand, fill our hearts, we beseech thee, with such love toward thee, that nothing may seem too hard for us to do and suffer in obedience to thy will; and grant that thus loving thee, we may become daily more like unto thee, and finally obtain the crown of life which thou hast promised to those that love thee; through Jesus Christ our Lord.

'Farnham Hostel Manual' (19th century)

Help me to grow
to love not only the poor,
not only anyone of any economic status or strata,
but to love the whole world,
all of creation—
from the minutest animal
to the greatest of men,
from the beginning to the end of eternity.

I think that my prayer
is much like
the story of an old monk who,
while, writing, looks up to the crucifix,
and the crucifix speaks to him.
And you were supposed to have said to him, Lord,
'Monk, what will you have of me?'
And he answered, 'Nothing but yourself, Lord'.
But, thinking about the context in which he asked,
I realized just a few nights ago
what he asked for.
There he looked up at you, hanging from the cross,
your arms outstretched, circling all of creation,
all of the world, all of the universe,
all of any kind of matter
and spirit,
everything,
all in all;
and when he asked for yourself,
he asked for all of this.
And if you ask me as you ask every one of us,
'Son, what do you wish of me?'
I say to you now, . . .
'Lord, nothing but yourself'.

Christopher William Jones

Peace

Deep peace from the Son of Peace,
Deep peace from the heart of Mary to you,
And from Bridget of the Mantle deep peace, deep
peace!

And with the kindness, too, of the Haughty
Father,
Peace!
In the name of the Three who are One, Peace!
And by the will of the King of the Elements,
Peace, Peace!

Alan Dall, translated by Fiona Macleod

Send down O God, O gentle, O compassionate,
into my heart faith and tranquillity and stillness,
that I may be of those whose 'hearts are tranquil-
lized by the mention of God'.

Muslim Prayer

O Lord, calm the waves of this heart; calm its
tempest! Calm thyself, O my soul, so that the divine
can act in thee! Calm thyself, O my soul, so that
God is able to repose in thee, so that his peace may
cover thee! Yes, Father in heaven, often have we
found that the world cannot give us peace. O but
make us feel that thou art able to give peace; let us
know the truth of thy promise: that the whole
world may not be able to take away thy peace.

Sören Kierkegaard (1813-1855)

O God of peace, who hast taught us that in
returning and in rest we shall be saved, and in
quietness and in confidence shall be our strength:
by the might of thy spirit lift us, we pray thee, to

thy presence, where we may be still and know that
thou art God; through Jesus Christ our Lord.

J. W. Suter

The peace of God, the peace of men,
The peace of Columba, kindly,
The peace of Mary mild, the loving,
The peace of Christ, King of Tenderness,
Be upon each window, upon each door,
Upon each hole that lets in the light,
Upon the four corners of my house,
Upon the four corners of my bed,
   Upon the four corners of my house,
   Upon the four corners of my bed;
Upon each thing my eye takes in,
Upon each thing my mouth takes in,
Upon my body that is of earth,
And upon my soul that came from on high;
   Upon my body that is of earth,
   And upon my soul that came from on high.

Alexander Carmichael

Joy

O God, who hast made the heaven and the earth
and all that is good and lovely therein, and hast
shown us through Jesus Christ our Lord that the
secret of joy is a heart free from selfish desires,
help us to find delight in simple things, and ever to
rejoice in the riches of thy bounty, through Jesus
Christ our Lord.

The Kingdom, the Power and the Glory

Grant me, O Lord, the royalty of inward happiness and the serenity which comes from living close to thee. Daily renew in me the sense of joy, and let the eternal spirit of the Father dwell in my soul and body, filling every corner of my heart with light and grace, so that bearing about with me the infection of a good courage, I may be a diffuser of life and may meet all ills and cross accidents with gallant and high-hearted happiness, giving thee thanks always for all things.

L. H. M. Soulsby (1856-1927)

Lord, you have sent me joy! I leap . . . I skip . . . it is good to be alive. You give life; you give the spirit of gladness to feed it. I love you. My sins are forgiven. It is good to be alive . . . and you have made it so.

Hubert van Zeller, OSB

VII

FORGIVENESS AND OPENING UP

Shot through prayer life, but intensifying at certain periods of development or circumstance, is the sense of sinfulness, rottenness, inadequacy in the face of God. No one who is growing in awareness and love of God can escape this sour and often harrowing self-realisation. And much as we might wish to put it on one side, we need to face it out— a truly humbling and purifying experience when it comes, and one which will recur. Saint Peter perhaps sensed this at the moment of seeing the power of Christ, when he cried out: 'Depart from me, for I am a sinful man.'

The world is particularly impervious to the idea of sin as it loses the idea of God. A generalised social conscience has however grown up, and many are plagued by the consciousness of the poverty, injustice and so on which are rampant throughout the land. These and other more personally directed twinges of conscience can hardly fail to get at the individual who is giving of his or her time and self to being alone with God, because this is part and parcel of the development of a two-way awareness

of God-self relationship and self-neighbour relationship.

The feeling may be general, or may be centred
on some aspect of your life which you know you
are always tripping up over, an area of self-
indulgence or neglect. It may be heightened by a
particularly bad lapse, such as would send a non-
believer to despair and suicide, and even a believer
almost as far.

The consciousness or feeling of sinfulness, inadequacy, rottenness may occur in a wide variety
of ways which depend on the individual and his
circumstances, and the way God chooses to approach him. This, of course, is true of everything
we can say about prayer, the variety of approach
and its timing is almost infinite. The sense of sin or
inadequacy or whatever it is may come at the very
beginning, when you have not yet approached God,
or have been so long away from him that your sense
is one of hopeless distance, of being beyond the
pale. Often I have heard people say: 'I'm too far
gone'. But here you must accept—ANYONE AT
ALL MUST ACCEPT—that you are not too far
gone, you cannot be this side of the grave, from
God's viewpoint. This is simply that you are weak
in faith and cannot yet accept God's infinite love
and mercy.

At the other end of the scale, the closer the soul
comes in union with God, the more anguishing and
at the same time the less specific is particular sin.
Yet somehow the more intense is the sense, in the

words of the author of the *Cloud of Unknowing* of being 'a lump of sin'.

This leads on to an intense desire for God to take over, where you know you are not strong enough, that he may open up the sore and let the pus out. Part of you says: 'Lord I love you so much' and another part says: 'You hypocrite! How can you say you love when you are so foul and selfish and alien to God?' And the other part says again: 'But Lord, I love you—I really do'. And so the heart and mind and self cries out to be taken, opened, purged, filled with love, and the 'I' cannot do anything about it except to offer and to suffer and to hope it is love—and somewhere to glimpse the love of God.

Forgiveness

Forgive me my sins, O Lord; the sins of my present and the sins of my past, the sins of my soul and the sins of my body, the sins which I have done to please myself and the sins which I have done to please others. Forgive my casual sins and my deliberate sins, and those which I have laboured so to hide that I have hidden them even from myself. Forgive me them, O Lord, forgive them all; for Jesus Christ's sake.

Thomas Wilson (1663-1775)

Set me free, Lord, from faith and hope in lesser things.

Set me free from commitment to my own blueprints for my own future.

Set me free for faith and hope in you.

Set me free for commitment to your plans for my future.

Set me free to live and work and serve, building your future.

Set me free, Lord, to be a man.

Rex Chapman

Lord Jesus, whereas I daily fall, and am ready to sin, vouchsafe me grace as often as I shall fall, to rise again; let me never presume, but always most meekly and humbly acknowledge my wretchedness and frailty, and repent with a firm purpose to

amend; let me not despair because of my great
frailty, but ever trust in thy most loving mercy and
readiness to forgive.

Robert Leighton (1611-1684)

Master, I daily betray thee,
Unworthy I am to kneel at thy feet;
Neither goodness is there, nor purity in me;
Nought but disloyalty, meanness, self-serving.
All things lie open to thee:
Dumbly I show thee the worst,
All my shame and sorrowful weakness,
All my baseness and cowardice, failure, folly and
    sin.
O Master, beautiful, stainless, and holy,
Thou knowest it all;
I am thine, take thou again
This worthless gift of my life,
Ah! take me again.
Only, Master, O Christ,
Only, I love thee so:
O Saviour, O Lover, O King
I love thee so.

J. S. Hoyland

   We let the world overcome us; we live too much
in continual fear of the chances and changes of
mortal life. We let things go too much their own
way. We try too much to get what we can by our
own selfish wits, without considering our neighbours. We follow too much the ways and fashions

of the day, doing and saying and thinking anything
that comes uppermost, just because there is so
much around us. Free us from our selfish interests,
and guide us, good Lord, to see your way, and to do
your will.

Charles Kingsley (1819-1875)

Superessential essence, nature uncreate,
   framer of the universe,
I set thee, Lord, before me,
   and to thee I lift up my soul:
I worship thee kneeling upon my knees,
   and I humble myself under thy mighty hand.
I stretch forth my hands,
   my soul gaspeth unto thee as a thirsty land:
I smite you my breast,
   and I say with the publican:
God be merciful to me the mere sinner,
   the chief of sinners.
To the sinner beyond the publican,
   be merciful as to the publican.

Lancelot Andrewes (1555-1626)

Out of the depths I cry to you, O Lord,
Lord, hear my voice!
O let your ears be attentive
to the voice of my pleading.
If you, O Lord, should mark our guilt,
Lord, who would survive?
But with you is found forgiveness;
for this we revere you.

My soul is waiting for the Lord,
I count on his word.
My soul is longing for the Lord
more than the watchman for daybreak.
Because with the Lord there is mercy
and fullness of redemption.
Israel indeed he will redeem
from all its iniquity.

Psalm 130

Forgive us the wrong we have done, as we forgive . . .

I have plenty of excuses, Lord, that I can produce at the drop of a hat.

Sometimes they convince others—a pity that they do not convince me.

Here is one:

I cannot be held responsible for all the wrong I do.

It is my upbringing, my parents' fault, not mine, someone else's bad influence.

Sometimes consciously, more often unconsciously, have they not shaped my personality so that I cannot be other than I am?

See that man over there, that man in prison, inadequate, unable to cope with his job, with his marriage, he drifted into petty larceny.

Was it really his fault?

He did not ask to be born into a substandard house.

He did not ask his father to fornicate and forget.

He did not ask his mother to fail in parenthood on her own.

Of course I have been luckier in life, in my background.

But is not the argument the same?

I cannot be responsible for all that I am, when I became what I am before being able to take responsibility.

It seems a good argument, Lord.

I wish it convinced me.

But I know that I am responsible.

I feel responsible.

Not to take responsibility is not to be a man.

It is good to know that I am not on my own.

It is we who are to be forgiven, not simply I.

Forgive us, forgive me, Lord, all that is less than it might have been, all failures in living.

Remove the guilt that inhibits life and action.

Your forgiveness revitalizes a man.

It frees him from his past, frees him to live and love, to be human for the future.

It restores his hope.

How can I experience this, Lord, if I do not do the same for my neighbour?

Rex Chapman

O Lord and Master of my life, take from me the spirit of sloth, faintheartedness, lust of power and idle talk. Give rather to me, thy servant, the spirit of chastity, humility, patience and love. Grant me, my Lord and King, to see my own errors and not to judge my brother for thou art blessed for ever and ever.

Saint Ephraem of Edessa (306-373)

O God, our Judge and Saviour, set before us the vision of thy purity and let us see our sins in the light of thy holiness. Pierce our self-contentment with the shafts of thy burning love, and let love consume in us all that hinders us from perfect service of thy cause; for thy holiness is our judgment, so are thy wounds our salvation.

William Temple (1881-1944)

I have sinned above the number of the sands of the sea, O Lord: my transgressions are multiplied, and I am not worthy to behold and see the height of heaven for the multitude of my iniquities.

I am bowed down with many iron bands, so that I cannot lift up my head, neither have I any respite: for I have provoked thy wrath, and done that which is evil before thee;

I did not thy will, neither kept I thy commandments.

Now therefore, I bow the knee of my heart, beseeching grace of thee.

I have sinned, and I acknowledge my iniquities: wherefore I humbly beseech thee, forgive me, O Lord, forgive me, and destroy me not with mine iniquities.

Be not angry with me for ever, for thou, O Lord, art the God of them that repent: and in me thou wilt show all thy goodness: for thou wilt save me, that am unworthy, according to thy great mercy.

And I will praise thee for ever all the days of my life: for all the host of heaven doth sing thy praise, and thine is the glory for ever and ever. Amen.

The Prayer of Manasses

Thou art my Lord, I thy servant. I have wronged myself and I confess my sin. Forgive me then all my sins, for there is none that forgiveth sins save thee.

Muhammed

Turn to me and forgive me with a forgiveness that shall make me forgive all but thee.

Muslim prayer

I ask thy forgiveness for every work which I had purposed to do for thee alone and into which I admitted human respect.

Muslim prayer

Have mercy upon me, O God, after thy great goodness; according to the multitude of thy mercies do away mine offences.

Wash me thoroughly from my wickedness; and cleanse me from my sin.

For I acknowledge my faults; and my sin is ever before me.

Against thee only have I sinned and done this evil in thy sight; that thou mightest be justified in thy saying, and clear when thou art judged.

Behold I was shaped in wickedness; and in sin hath my mother conceived me.

But lo, thou requirest truth in my inward parts; and shalt make me to understand wisdom secretly.

Thou shalt purge me with hyssop, and I shall be clean; thou shalt wash me and I shall be whiter than snow.

Turn thy face from my sins, and put out all my misdeeds.

Make me a clean heart, O God; and renew a right spirit within me.

Cast me not away from thy presence; and take not thy Holy Spirit from me.

O give me the comfort of thy help again; and establish me with thy free Spirit.

O Lord open thou my lips, and my mouth shall shew forth thy praise.

Psalm 51

We who stand in the world offer ourselves and our society for your blessed healing.

We confess we have failed to love as you did.

We have been socially unjust, and our society is imperfect, fragmented, and sometimes sick to death.

Teach us your ways in the world and in this life which we share together.

Don't let us restrict you to a narrow ghetto

labelled 'religion', but lead us to worship you in the fulness of life as the lord of politics, economics and the arts.

Give us light to seek true morality, not in narrow legalisms but in sacrifice and open responsibility. Show us how to express our love for you in very specific, human service to other men.

Lord, change our hearts from hearts of stone to hearts of flesh, and let us give thanks to you for all of life.

Malcolm Boyd

Nothing, I am nothing, I accomplished nothing,
    I know it now.
Your light is hard, merciless, Lord.
No corner of my life and soul remains in the
    shadow.
Turn as I may, your light is everywhere,
And I stand naked and full of fear.
Formerly I admitted that I was a sinner, that I
    was unworthy,
And I believed it, Lord, but I didn't know it.
In your presence I looked for some faults
But produced only laboured and feeble con-
    fessions.
Lord, it is my whole being that kneels now,
It's the sin that I am that asks forgiveness.
Lord, thank you for your light—I would never
    have known,
But Lord, enough. I assure you I've understood.

I am nothing
And you are all.

Michel Quoist

Opening-up: the part of love

O Lord our God, grant us grace to desire thee
with a whole heart, so that desiring thee we may
seek and find thee; and so finding thee, may love
thee; and loving thee, may hate those sins which
separate us from thee, for the sake of Jesus Christ.

Saint Anselm (1033-1109)

Make us receptive and open
and may we accept your kingdom
like children taking bread
from the hands of their father.
Let us live in your peace,
at home with you
all the days of our lives.

Huub Oosterhuis

Lord teach us how to be open to your Spirit. We
want to know your will and to do it, but it is difficult to recognise in this bewildering world. Our
occupations and our desires for ourselves prevent
us from being open. Help us to put away all
thoughts and self-preoccupations which hinder the
action of your Spirit and deter us from being
responsive to him. We so often think that we know

what is right and do not give you a chance to show us your will. Lord, make us receptive to your comings to us. Help us to put away self-deception so that we may grow in wisdom and love.

Etta Gullick

Lord Jesus Christ, you have revealed yourself to us, and in this way have revealed your Father also. But our minds and hearts are slow to believe and love. Open us, Lord, to the wonder of your manhood; stir us to the following of your example; urge us to the realization of your life here on earth in terms of our living, that we may truly live for our fellow human beings and so live for you, who are God for ever and ever.

Michael Hollings

O my God, thou hast wounded me with love,
Behold the wound that is still vibrating.
O my God, thou hast wounded me with love.
O my God, thy fear hath fallen upon me,
Behold the burn is there and throbs aloud.
O my God, thy fear hath fallen upon me.
O my God, I have known all that is vile,
And thy glory hath stationed itself in me,
O my God, I have known all that is vile.
Take my blood that I have not poured out,
Take my flesh unworthy of thy suffering,
Take my blood that I have not poured out . . .

Take my heart that has beaten for vain things,
To throb under the thorns of Calvary.
Take my heart that has beaten for vain things.
Ah, thou God of pardon and promises,
What is the pit of mine ingratitude!
Ah, thou God of pardon and promises.
God of terror and God of holiness,
Alas, my sinfulness is a black abyss,
God of terror and holiness.
Thou God of peace, of joy and delight,
All my tears, all my ignorances,
Thou God of peace, of joyous delight.
Thou, God, knowest all this, all this,
How poor I am, poorer than any man,
Thou, O God, knowest all this, all this.
And what I have, my God, I give to thee.

Paul Verlaine (1844-1896),
translated by Arthur Symons

Lord Jesus Christ, that we may be able rightly to
pray thee for all things, we pray first for one; help
us to love thee much, increase love and inflame it.
Oh, this is a prayer thou wilt surely hear, thou who
indeed art not love of such a sort—so cruel a sort—
that thou art only the object, indifferent as to
whether anyone loves thee or not; thou indeed art
not love of such a sort—in wrath—that thou art
only judgment, jealous of who loves thee and who
does not. Oh, no, such a sort thou art not; thou
wouldst thus only inspire fear and dread and it
would then be terrible to come to thee, frightful

to abide with thee, and thou wouldst not be perfect
love which casteth out fear. No, compassionate,
loving or in love, thou art love of such a sort that
thou thyself dost woo forth the love which loves
thee, dost foster it to love thee much.

Sören Kierkegaard (1813-1855)

Lord, thou knowest that I love thee: John 21, 16

You know better than I how much I love you,
Lord. You know it and I know it not, for nothing
is more hidden from me than the depths of my own
heart. I desire to love you; I fear that I do not love
you enough. I beseech you to grant me the fulness
of pure love. Behold my desire; you have given it
to me. Behold in your creature what you have
placed there. O God, who love me enough to
inspire me to love you for ever, behold not my sins.
Behold your mercy and my love.

François Fénelon (1651-1715)

Lord, I believe in thee; help thou mine unbelief.
I love thee, yet not with a perfect heart as I would;
I trust in thee, yet not with my whole mind. Accept
my faith, my love, my longing to know and serve
thee, my trust in thy power to keep me. What is
cold, do thou kindle, what is lacking, do thou
make up. I wait thy blessing through Jesus Christ
our Lord.

Malcolm Spencer

O God, my God and my all,
without thee I am nothing, less than nothing,
a rebel to thy love,
a despiser of thy grace.
O God have pity on me a sinner;
grant me a new vision of thy love
and of thy will for me;
give me a stillness in my soul
that I may know thee and love thee,
and grant me strength to do thy will, O my God,
    my all.

Gilbert Shaw

Jesus, may I by the repetition of thy name
be drawn to thee so close
in worshipping response
to hold thee still,
that I may know the living quiet of thy love,
the love that passeth understanding.

Gilbert Shaw

Set our hearts on fire with love to thee, O Christ
Our God, that in that flame we may love thee with
all our hearts, with all our mind, with all our soul,
and with all our strength, and our neighbours as
ourselves; so that, keeping thy commandments,
we may glorify thee, the giver of all good gifts.

Eastern Orthodox Prayer

Opening up: our part

O Emmanuel, O Wisdom, I give myself to thee,
I trust thee wholly. Thou art wiser than I, more
loving to me than I am to myself; deign to fulfil
thy high purposes in me, whatever they be. Work in
and through me: I am born to serve thee, to be
thine, to be thy instrument. Let me be thy blind
instrument. I ask not to see, I ask not to know,
I ask simply to be used.

J. H. Newman (1801-1890)

Lord, I have prayed so long,
'My will be done',
Yet thou hast gentle been,
Thou hast not judged my wrong,
But waited till I'd won
Thought more serene.
Alas! O Lord not yet
Can I lay claim
To find surrender dear.
Yet would I leave my fret
Or think of it with shame,
Since thou art near.
But, giving all, I learn
That nothing's lost
And only given so.
Then do thou help me turn
And wish, whate'er the cost,
My overthrow.

Norman Hunt

Take, Lord, all my liberty. Receive my memory, my understanding, and my whole will. Whatever I have and possess, thou hast given me; to thee I restore it wholly, and to thy will I utterly surrender it for my direction. Give me the love of thee only, with thy grace, and I am rich enough; nor ask I anything beside.

Saint Ignatius of Loyola (1491-1556)

Preserve me thy servant from all evil, lead me into all good; change my sorrows into comforts, my infirmity into spiritual strength; take all iniquity from me, and let thy servant never depart from thee. I am thine, O save me; I am thine, sanctify and preserve me for ever; that neither life nor death, health nor sickness, prosperity nor adversity, weakness within nor cross accidents without, may ever separate me from the love of God which is in Christ Jesus our Lord.

Jeremy Taylor (1613-1667)

Use me, my Saviour, for whatever purpose and in whatever way thou mayest require. Here is my poor heart, an empty vessel; fill it with thy grace. Here is my sinful, troubled soul; quicken it and refresh it with thy love. Take my heart for thine abode; my mouth to spread abroad the glory of thy name; my love and all my powers for the advancement of thy believing people, and never

suffer the steadfastness and confidence of my faith
to abate.

Dwight Moody (1837-1899)

Sever me from myself that I may be grateful unto
    thee;
May I perish to myself that I may be safe in thee;
May I die to myself that I may live in thee;
May I wither to myself that I may blossom in
    thee;
May I be emptied of myself that I may abound in
    thee;
May I be nothing to myself that I may be all to
    thee.

Desiderius Erasmus (1466-1536)

O King of kings!
O sheltering wings, O guardian tree!
All, all of me,
Thou Virgin's nurseling! rests in thee.

Translated from the Irish by Robin Flower

God be in my head,
And in my understanding.
God be in my eyes,
And in my looking.
God be in my mouth,
And in my speaking.
God be in my heart,
And in my thinking.

God be in mine end,
And at my departing.

Sarum Primer (1527)

Take my will and make it thine
It shall be no longer mine.
Take my heart: it is thine own!
It shall be thy royal throne.
Take my love; my Lord I pour
at thy feet its treasure store.
Take myself, and I will be
Ever, only, all for thee.

Frances R. Havergal (1836-1879)

Lord, of thy goodness, give me thyself, for only in thee have I all.

O Lord, starve what is 'me' in me; nourish what is thou! Blood of Christ wash me white and intoxicate my insensitiveness.

Anonymous

Well, I don't feel perfectly free. I don't feel free at all. I am captive to myself.

I do what I want. I have it all my own way. There is no freedom at all for me in this, Jesus. Today I feel like a slave bound in chains and branded by a hot iron because I am captive to my own will and I don't give an honest damn about you or your will.

You're over there where I'm keeping you, outside my real life. How can I go on being such a lousy hypocrite? Come over here, where I don't want you to come. Let me quit playing this blasphemous game of religion with you. Jesus, help me to let you be yourself in my life—so that I may be myself.

Malcolm Boyd

Opening up: God's part

Our God, who art our winged self, it is thy will
in us that willeth.
It is thy desire in us that desireth.
It is thy urge in us that would turn our nights
which are thine, into days which are thine also.
We cannot ask thee for aught, for thou knowest
our needs before they are born in us;
thou art our need, and in giving us more of
thyself,
thou givest us all.

Kahil Gibran

Batter at my heart, three-person'd God, for you
as yet but knock! Breathe, shine and seek to mend;
that I may rise and stand, o'erthrow me, and bend
your force to break, blow, burn, and make me new.
I, like an usurp'd town, to another due
labour to admit you, but O, to no end!
Reason, your viceroy in me, me should defend,
but is captiv'd and proves weak or untrue.

Yet dearly I love you, and would be loved fain,
but am betrothed unto your enemy;
divorce me, untie, or break that knot again,
take me to you, imprison me, for I
except you enthral me, never shall be free,
nor ever chaste, except you ravish me.

John Donne (1572-1631)

Lord:
Are your demands reasonable? They are excessive
for a man on his own. Can I stand the pace? It
remains to be seen.
Lord, lead me to your activity in the world,
Lead me along the Via Dolorosa, the way of the
cross.
But I need your support to bear the weight of the
cross I have to shoulder.
You carried yours.
This encourages me to take the plunge again and
again.
Sometimes I feel like the man with the foundation
laid, but left unfinished like a ruin.
Sometimes you succeed through me; you finish the
job.

I am yours, Lord.
Make me yours.

Rex Chapman

O God! O God! We ask that thou wilt turn away
our faces from any other goal than thyself, and

grant us to gaze toward thy noble countenance
until we see thee in everything.

Muslim prayer

O God, who madest me for thyself to show forth
thy goodness in me; manifest, I humbly beseech
thee, the life-giving power of thy holy nature within
me; help me to such a true and living faith in thee,
such strength of hunger and thirst after the birth,
life and spirit of thy holy Jesus in my soul, that all
that is within me may be turned from every inward
thought or outward work that is not thee, thy holy
Jesus, and heavenly workings in my soul.

William Law (1689-1761)

Work within me, within us, within the Church.
Be at the centre of our lives.
Mould us in your image.
Bring about our transformation.
Make us fruitful, Lord,
　　　　Now,
Here as well as there,
Me as well as the others.

Rex Chapman

Lord, bestow on me two gifts,
　　—to forget myself
　　—never to forget thee.
Keep me from self-love, self-pity, self-will
　　in every guise and disguise

nor ever let me measure myself by myself.
Save me from self,
> my tempter, seducer, jailer;
> corrupting desire at the spring,
> closing the avenues of grace,
> leading me down the streets of death.
Rather, let my soul devote to thee
> its aspirations, affections, resolutions.
Let my mind look unto thee
> in all its searchings, shinings, certitudes.
Let my body work for thee
> with its full health and abilities.
Let thy love pass
> into the depth of my heart,
> into the heart of my prayer,
> into the heart of my whole being;
So that I desert myself
> and dwell and move in thee
> in peace, now and evermore.

Eric Milner White

My Lord and my God—
thank you for drawing me to yourself.
Make me desire more deeply
that knowledge of you which is eternal life.
Lord,
you have told us that the pure in heart shall see God
—the single-minded
who do not try to serve two masters,
who have no other gods but you.
Keep the burning of my desire for you

as clear and steady as the flame of a candle,
—a single, undivided focus of attention,
a steady offering of the will.
Let my whole being be filled with your light
so that others may be drawn to you.
Let my whole being be cleansed by the flame of your
  love
from all that is contrary to your will for me,
from all that keeps others from coming to you.
Let my whole being be consumed in your service,
so that others may know your love,
—my Lord and my God.

Margaret Dewey

Yea, Lord Jesus Christ, whether we be far off or near, far away from thee in the human swarm, in business, in earthly cares, in temporal joys, in merely human highness, or far from all this, forsaken, unappreciated in lowliness, and with this the nearer to thee, do thou draw us, draw us entirely to thyself.

Sören Kierkegaard

O Saviour, pour upon me thy spirit of meekness and love, annihilate the selfhood in me, be thou all my life. Guide thou my hand which trembles exceedingly upon the rock of ages.

William Blake (1757-1827)

O Lord! Throw me not on myself: of my will I can not speak nor observe silence.

Throw me not on my own strength: of my will I can not pray nor give myself to thee!

Nor can I follow life nor even death!

Not by my own power can I a beggar be, or a king!

Throw me not on myself, for by myself I cannot gain my soul nor the knowledge of thyself.

Throw me not on myself, for I am unable to cross the sea of change.

I cannot, O Lord!

Guru Nanak

Be thou my vision, O Lord of my heart,
Be all else but naught to me, save that thou art;
Be thou my best thought in the day and the night,
Both waking and sleeping, thy presence my light.
Be thou my wisdom, be thou my true word,
Be thou ever with me, and I with thee, Lord;
Be thou my great Father, and I thy true son;
Be thou in me dwelling, and I with thee one.
Be thou my breastplate, my sword for the fight;
Be thou my whole armour, be thou my true might;
Be thou my soul's shelter, be thou my strong tower;
O raise thou me heavenward, great power of my
    power.
Riches I heed not, nor man's empty praise;
Be thou mine inheritance now and always;
Be thou and thou only the first in my heart:
O sovereign of heaven, my treasure thou art.

High king of heaven, thou heaven's bright sun
O grant me its joys after vict'ry is won;
Great heart of my own heart, whatever befall,
Still be thou my vision, O ruler of all.

Irish (8th century);
translated by Mary Byrne (1880-1931);
versified Eleanor Hull (1860-1935)

Teach us, our God and king,
In all things thee to see,
That what we do in anything
We do it unto thee.

George Herbert (1593-1633)

Be thou a light unto my eyes, music to mine
ears, sweetness to my taste, and full contentment
to my heart. Be thou my sunshine in the day, my
food at table, my repose in the night, my clothing in
nakedness, and my succour in all necessities. Lord
Jesu, I give thee my body, my soul, my substance,
my fame, my friends, my liberty and my life.
Dispose of me and all that is mine as it may seem
best to thee and to the glory of thy blessed name.

John Cosin (1594-1672)

Lord, teach us to understand that your Son died
to save us, not from suffering, but from ourselves;
not from injustice, far less from justice, but from
being unjust. He died that we might live—but live
as he lives, by dying as he died who died to himself.

George Macdonald (1824-1905)

My prayers, my God, flow from what I am not,
I think thy answers make me what I am.
Like weary waves thought flows upon thought,
But the still depth beneath is all thine own,
And there thou mov'st in paths to us unknown.
Out of strange strife thy peace is strangely
      wrought.
If the lion in us pray—thou answerest the lamb.

George Macdonald (1824-1905)

O my most dear Lord, I will have nothing in my
memory but thee, my Lord and God, my very
original, in whom I was from the beginning.
Neither will I have anything in my understanding
but thee only and all creatures in thee. Neither will
I have in my will and desire any other thing but the
execution and doing of thy most holy will.

William Perin (died 1557)

Teach us stillness and confident peace
In thy perfect will—
Deep calm of soul and content
In what thou will do with these lives thou hast given.
Teach us to wait and be still
To rest in thyself,
To hush this clamorous anxiety,
To lay in thine arms all this wealth thou hast given.
Thou lovest these souls that we love
With a love as far surpassing our own

As the glory of the moon surpasses the gleam of a
candle.
Therefore will we be still and trust in thee.

J. S. Hoyland

Like as the heart desireth the waterbrooks, so
longeth my soul after thee, O God.
My soul is athirst for God, yea, even for the living
God; when shall I come to appear before the presence of God?

Psalm 42

O God, thou art my God: early will I seek thee.
My soul thirsteth for thee, my flesh also longeth
after thee, in a barren and dry land where no water
is.
For thy loving kindness is better than life itself:
my lips shall praise thee.
As long as I live I will magnify thee on this
manner: and lift up my hands in thy name.
Have I not remembered thee in my bed: and
thought upon thee when I was waking.
Because thou hast been my helper, therefore
under the shadow of thy wings will I rejoice.

Psalm 63

VIII

DARKNESS AND UNBELIEF

The term 'darkness' is one which comes at different stages and has different meanings. It is, however, very much a part of growth in prayer, and needs to be looked at, if not fully understood. Why? Because if you are going to go on, you will need to go through it, and let it go through you.

In the beginning, there may be the darkness which is really blankness—unbelief. The soul can be shattered from God's light, not knowing how to begin to pray, not even wanting to, or thinking it possible. Faced with this impossibility, the impossible is demanded; you must 'Begin, all the same' . . . somehow, anyhow, however falteringly, however little.

When a person has set off in rather a different mood—filled with joy and eagerness, the honeymoon period which seems so full of light and promise gives way in most cases to loss of light, greyness and aridity. It is not quite dark, but it is like those days when a blight comes over the weather and nothing is quite so good or so worth while. The difficulty at that point is to avoid going back or trying to do so, starting all over again, trying to recapture the first taste of God which was so good. But this is the one thing you must not do, for it is necessary to go on through it—not back.

Later there may be a deeper darkness as you move into the unknown—a loss of images, an intensification of aridity. Again this, though difficult and even painful and tasteless, like eating sawdust while you pray, must be gone through. It is right, however wrong it feels; so keep on. You may be partly experiencing that God is immense— that is, too big for your mind to grasp or focus upon, and therefore everything blurs, becomes indistinct. Perhaps, too, in the greater penetration of God's light into the soul there must ensue darkness, as happens with the naked eye moving from darkness to sudden sunshine.

There is another darkness (or is it part of the same? Who knows!). This is desolation. It can be a sense of the loss of God or of sin separating you from God; when it is really bad, it can seem that God is abandoning you. In some cases the intensity grows to the point where the horror and blackness of it stems from the idea that God hates you and appears to will your destruction. When God is lost, then faith is deeply tested. It is not at all unusual—in fact it is to be expected—that you seem no longer able to believe that God exists.

Needless to say, much of this is very painful and almost puts the soul into a panic. There is genuine need for a guide at these times—even if only to give support and encouragement to go on. It can appear to be a real agony. Only God fully knows the purpose of it. But the soul, which is humble enough to endure in faith, later glimpses what it is all about—but only later.

The message at these points is to live through, groan, let yourself be broken open or be ignored by God. Above all, trust.

Dear God,

I am rather hesitant about addressing anything at all to you just now. Faith is hard for all of us in these days, and I've been having a pretty dark patch lately. But if I believe in anything I believe in your love, so please increase that trust till I am certain that whatever I do I can't stop you loving me.

It is a relief to realise that you know exactly how I feel, what I can say honestly, and what I wish I could say, but can't just now. So on this basis I am able to finish quite honestly by saying,

With love,
from Bill

Prayer of an undergraduate

Ah Lord, my prayers are dead, my affections dead, and my heart is dead: but thou art a living God and I bear myself upon thee.

William Bridge (1600-1670)

I wish, God, for some end I do not will.
Between the fire and heart a veil of ice
Puts out the fire. My pen will not move well
So that the sheet on which I'm working lies.
I pay you mere lip-service, then I grieve;
Love does not reach my heart, I do not know
How to admit that grace which should relieve
My state and crush the arrogance I show.
O tear away that veil, God, break that wall

147

Which with its strength refuses to let in
The sun whose light has vanished from the world.
Send down the promised light to bless and hold
Your lovely bride. So may I seek for all
I need in you, both end there and begin.

Sonnets of Michelangelo,
translated by Elizabeth Jennings

O my Lord, I am in a dry land, all dried up and cracked by the violence of the north wind and the cold; but as thou seest, I ask for nothing more; thou wilt send me both dew and warmth when it pleaseth thee.

Saint Jane de Chantal (1572-1641)

Lord, since thou hast taken from all that I had of thee, yet of thy grace leave the gift which every dog has by nature: that of being true to thee in my distress, when I am deprived of all consolation. This I desire more fervently than thy heavenly kingdom!

Saint Mechthild of Magdeburg (c. 1210-1280)

Speak Lord, for thy servant heareth (1 Samuel 3, 9)

I am silent, Lord, in my affliction. I am silent. In the stillness of a contrite and humble heart, I listen to you. Lord, see my wounds; you have made them. You have smitten me. I am silent; I suffer. I worship silently. Yet you hear my sighs, and the lamentations of my heart are not hidden from you.

Let me not listen to myself. I long to hear your
voice and to follow you.

François Fénelon (1651-1715)

Lord give us grace to hold to thee
when all is weariness and fear
and sin abounds within, without,
when that I would do I cannot do
and that I do I would not do,
when love itself is tested by the doubt
that love is false or dead within the soul,
when every act brings new confusion, new
    distress,
new opportunities, new misunderstandings,
and every thought new accusation.
Lord give us grace
that we may know that in the darkness pressing
    round
it is the mist that hides thy face;
that thou art there
and thou dost know we love thee still.

Gilbert Shaw

Lord, even you know what it's like to feel as if
    'God is no more', to wonder if what you've
    staked your whole life on is after all just an
    illusion.
You know what it is like to keep going in the dark
    by a sheer act of will; to go on loving when
    there seems to be no response; to abandon

oneself to a divine providence one can neither see nor feel.

Lord, when it's dark and we can't feel your presence, and nothing seems real any more, and we're tempted to give up trying—help us to know that you are never really absent—that we are like a little child in its mother's arms, held so close to your heart that we cannot see your face, and that underneath are the everlasting arms.

Margaret Dewey

God, this word we call you by
is almost dead and meaningless,
transient and empty
like all the words men use.
We ask you
to renew its force and meaning,
to make it once again
a name that brings your promise to us.
Make it a living word
which tells us
that you will be for us
as you have always been—
trustworthy and hidden
and very close to us,
Our God, now and for ever.

Huub Oosterhuis

He whom I bow to knows to whom I bow when
I attempt the ineffable name, murmuring Thou,
and dream of Phridian fancies and embrace in heart
symbols (I know) which cannot be the thing thou
    art.
Thus always, taken at their word, all prayers
    blaspheme,
worshipping with frail images a folk-lore dream,
and all men in their praying self-deceived, address
the coinage of their own unquiet thoughts, unless
thou in magnetic mercy to thyself divert
our arrows, aimed unskilfully beyond desert;
and all men are idolators, crying unheard
to a deaf idol, if thou take them at their word.
Take not, O Lord, our literal sense. Lord, in thy
great unbroken speech our limping metaphor
translate.

C. S. Lewis

Lord, where are you?
I've searched everywhere,
but still cannot find you.
In fact, I've searched the exchange,
but they couldn't put me thru' . . .
They said their books could not
contain your number;
so what am I to do?
Or, are you even there?
Are you in my neighbour,
or in the thing at which I stare?
Oh, Lord, where are you?

I even went as far as to put
a police-message for them to find you.
But Lord—they cannot find you.
We've all searched—everywhere.
Then, at last, I thought I had you,
but . . . Lord, you were not there,
or . . . were you?

*From 'Lord, make me truly human', Teenagers'
prayers from Saint John's High School, Salisbury,
Rhodesia*

Lord,
You gave man the world for his own.
You gave him a free will . . . and yet you are
guiding him to do the right things.
I, as a teenager, know that I can be independent,
but I also know that this independence and freedom
which you give every person, must be used
in a correct way.
I want to fight against authority,
to show that I have a mind of my own.
I want to show the adults
that I can be good.
Sometimes, God, I know you are there,
but I fight you.
Yet, I still know that there is a limit
to my independence,
that I can never be entirely free,
because you are a great God, and

will always be there.
Yes, God . . . I can never avoid you.

From 'Lord, make me truly human', Teenagers'
prayers from Saint John's High School, Salisbury,
Rhodesia

O Christ, my Lord, again and again I have said
with Mary Magdalene, 'They have taken away my
Lord and I know not where they have laid him'.
I have been desolate and alone. And thou hast
found me again, and I know that what has died is
not thou, my Lord, but only my idea of thee, the
image which I have made to preserve what I have
found, and to be my security. I shall make another
image, O Lord, better than the last. That too must
go, and all successive images, until I come to the
blessed vision of thyself, O Christ, my Lord.

George Appleton

Ah my dear angry Lord,
Since thou dost love, yet strike;
Cast down, yet help afford;
Sure I will do the like.
I will complain, yet praise;
I will bewail, approve;
And my sour-sweet days
I will lament, and love.

George Herbert (1593-1633)

Lord, thou hast led me astray, and I have followed thy leading; thou wast the stronger and thou hast prevailed. I heard thee say: 'Come unto me, all ye that labour and are heavy laden, and I will refresh you.' I came to thee and trusted thy word, and in what way hast thou refreshed me? I was not in labour before, but I am labouring now, and ready to drop with toil. I have looked all around but there is none to help me, and I have sought but there is none to give me aid.

Lord: You complain that I do not refresh you. Had I not refreshed you, you would have fainted away. The thing which makes the sweetness of my yoke, the lightness of my burden, is charity. If you had charity, then you would feel that sweetness.

Answer: Lord I have done what I could. My wretched body I have handed over to thy service. If thou dost not bestow charity, then I have not got it; and if I may not have it, I cannot go on. Thou knowest and seest how little I can do. Take of that little whatsoever thou wilt, and give me that entire and perfect charity.

Lord: Am I then to supply your deficiencies and give you the charity for which you ask so well? But you must accept my chastening. There is no going except by the *Way*. You must follow as you see me go before. I suffered many things, it behoves you to suffer some too. But you must recognise how great a thing is charity and worthy to be bought at a high price. For God is charity, and when you reach that, you will labour no more.

Answer: I dare not ask to be relieved of labour, nor do I want to do so; but in the meantime, while I have not got charity, who is going to bear the toil along with me?

Lord: I have made and I will bear. You have already been given a measure of charity, but you either do not know it, or are ungrateful for it . . . .

Answer: Truly, O Lord, thou hast become our refuge: to thee have I fled; teach me thy will and make me do it . . . I am thine: O save me. Into thy hands I commend my spirit. By thy grace I will not forsake thee.

William of Saint Thierry (1085-1148)

Lord, am I losing my mind?
Or is this what you want?
It would not matter, except that I am alone,
                              I am alone.
You have taken me far, Lord; trusting I followed
    you, and you walked by my side.
And now, at night, in the middle of the desert,
                    suddenly you have disappeared.
I call, and you do not answer.
I search, and I do not find you.
I left everything, and now am left alone,
Your absence is my suffering.
Lord it is dark.

Lord, are you here in my darkness?
Where are you, Lord?
Do you love me still?
Or have I wearied you?

> Lord, answer,
> Answer.
> It is dark.

Michel Quoist

IX

SHORT PRAYERS

There has been a long tradition of the use of short or ejaculatory prayers. They are endlessly varied and almost as endlessly useful. Men and women of prayer have had much used favourites. They can be drawn from the Bible, from the saints, from life, from you. They can express anything from joy to desolation, from praise to a plea for faith.

Method of use may be deliberately developed, to assist the development of your consciousness of God as you move about your daily round. Those who have been of a certain 'school' have set themselves the task of repeating so many ejaculations per hour. Not unlike this is the Jesus Prayer of the Orthodox, where the same short prayer is said over and over again. For some, the way in to this form, is to make a point of not saying so many per hour, but rather of turning to God at set times. For instance, a woman might do so each time she lit the gas or electric cooker, made a bed, potted the baby; a man might when he fetched in the coal, dug the garden, got on or off a bus, clocked in and out at work, wrote a letter, parked the car.

Gradually these short prayers should weave a pattern in your life, so that from something imposed on an unwilling nature they grow to be 'natural' unforced and spontaneous. In fact they are as simple as breathing and need no more concentration than that.

Indeed another word used for this kind of prayer is 'aspiration' and somewhere far back has something to do with breathing . . . it is as it were the unvoiced desire, the unvoiced plea for help, the unvoiced sigh of love.

It may be seen to follow from this that the length between short prayers may extend until almost unconsciously the short prayer dies out, except for the occasional burst, because silence has grown and silence begins to fill what before had to be filled with sound or at least a briefly expressed 'reminder'. The silence is not empty but is full of God, of the peace of God, or it seems a loss of you in God—it is hard to describe but it can be still and wonderful. Let the silence grow. Do not try to keep up the increasingly unnecessary ejaculations.

Lord Jesus Christ, Son of God, have mercy on me, a sinner.

Eastern Orthodox 'Jesus' prayer

Lord make speed to save us,
God make haste to help us.

Psalm 70:1

Make me thine own, till there is no lordship in my life but thine.

Muslim prayer

Thou, Lord, art the strength of my life; of whom shall I be afraid?

Psalm 27:1

O Lord, send out thy light and thy truth; let them lead me.

Psalm 43:3

O my God, how near thou art to me, and how far I am from thee.

Muslim prayer

O God, grant me courage, gaiety of spirit and tranquillity of mind.

R. L. Stevenson

Lord, give me what you are requiring of me.

Saint Augustine

O Lord, put no trust in me, for I shall surely fall if thou upholdest me not.

Saint Philip Neri

Praise the Lord, O my soul, and all that is within me, bless his holy name.

Psalm 103, verse 1

Lord I believe, help thou my unbelief.

Mark 9: 24

Lord, direct our hearts into the love of God.

2 Thessalonians 3:5

Lord, I am hopeless and helpless, help me.

Speak Lord, thy servant heareth.

1 Samuel 3:10

Come, Lord Jesus, come.

Lord, that I may see.

Lord, who hast given all for us, help us to give all for tnee.

G. W. Biggs

With you all things are possible.

Father, forgive them for they know not what they do.

Luke 23:34

Lord, without you I can do nothing.

My God, let me only love and that suffices me.

Augustine Baker (1575-1641)

Teach me to pray, pray thou thyself in me.

François Fénelon (1651-1715)

O God, make us children of quietness and heirs of peace.

Saint Clement (150-215)

Be still and know that I am God.

Psalm 46:10

Father, into thy hands I commend my spirit.

Luke 23:46

Lord come to me, my door is open.

Michel Quoist

Lord, of thy goodness, give me thy self.

Crucify me that you may be.

Nothing but Jesus, nothing but Jesus.

Augustine Baker (1575-1641)

All shall be well, and all manner of thing shall be well.

Lady Julian of Norwich

Lord, thou knowest that I love thee.

John 21:16

Not my will, thy will be done.

Luke 22:42

Be it unto me according to thy word.

Luke 1:38

Nought for me, all for thee.

O Lord, my strength and my redeemer.

Psalm 19:14

My Lord and my God.

John 20:28

My God and my all.

Saint Francis of Assisi (1181-1226)

Lord, though thou slay me yet will I trust thee.

after Job 13:15

My God, my God, why hast thou forsaken me?

Matthew 27:46

Help!
Jesus!
Lord!

X

TAKING OFF PRAYERS

This may sound a silly phrase, but it implies a change of mood and texture in prayer. It might be summed up in the frustration and feeling of being held back which is in Saint Paul's 'who will rid me of this body of death?' There grows a yearning to be 'better at prayer', to be more deeply involved in Christ, to cut out distractions, to by-pass the fetters of the mind, to take off from the pedestrian grind of prayer—to be air-borne.

The movement of escape is also a hushing or stilling. In a busy world in which you are busy, you become conscious of the still immensity of God. You wish to be steeped in it, and the 'giddy little butterfly of the mind' most tiresomely flits about and will not rest. You know with part of you that if only you could enter the silence of God, you would hear the voice of God, but the imagination is restive.

In another way, there are times of prayer when time ceases. You are 'caught' and 'held' by God. The experience is not easy—perhaps not possible— to explain, but like a small child raised high in its parent's arms and then put down—you cry out with all your being—'again—do it again'.

Sometimes it seems that the still, quiet prayer fulfils all the longings of the soul, the end of all desiring is reached. Yet somehow, though all desire is fulfilled and the soul is content and at peace, it longs even more for God whose immensity always seems beyond its reach or capacity.

Some of these prayers prepare us, still us, encourage our yearnings. But filled with the Spirit, we have to learn patience and humbly accept that this is God's part—not ours. As we know God is love, so we are prepared lovingly to wait on God.

Almost any short prayer or verse of a psalm may be used as a 'taking-off' prayer. The following short prayers, however, may be found helpful.

Be still and see that I am God.

Lord, that I may see.

Lord, thou knowest all things, thou knowest that
I love thee.

Rabboni—master.

Jesus.

Come, Lord Jesus.

Lord, you are hopeless, you flood me and you
empty me.

Now I am empty, and grey inside. But, Lord,
here I am.

'I look at him and he looks at me'.

> *(A French peasant when asked what he did
> sitting at the back of a church).*

Do thou, O friend, push on bodily to the mystic
vision, abandon the work of the senses and the
operations of the reasoning faculty, leave aside all
things visible and invisible, being and non-being,
and cleave as far as is possible, and imperceptibly, to
the unity of him who transcends all essences and
all knowledge. In this immeasurable and absolute
elevation of soul, forgetting all created things and

liberated from them, thou shalt rise above thyself and beyond all creation to find thyself within the shaft of light that flashes out from the divine, mysterious darkness.

But if thou wouldst know how such things are accomplished, then ask grace, not learning; desire, not understanding; the groanings of prayer, not industry in study; the spouse not the master; God, not man; obscurity, not clarity. Seek not so much light as fire which enflames one totally, filling the soul with unction and ardent desires, and rising out of its very self aloft to God. This fire is indeed God, whose 'furnace is in Jerusalem'. It was kindled on earth by the Man Jesus, in the fervour of his most ardent passion. In this fervour he participates who can say: 'My soul has chosen strangling and my bones death'. He shall see God who chooses such a death, for it is undoubtedly true that 'man shall not see me and live'. Let us die, therefore, and by the door of death enter into this darkness. Let us impose silence on our anxieties, our concupiscences, and upon the workings of our imagination. Let us, with Christ crucified, pass from this world to the Father, that when it shall be revealed to us we may say with Philip: 'It is enough for us'.

Saint Bonaventure (1221-1274)

In order to arrive at having pleasure in everything,
Desire to have pleasure in nothing.

In order to arrive at possessing everything,
Desire to possess nothing.
In order to arrive at being everything,
Desire to be nothing.
In order to arrive at knowing everything,
Desire to know nothing.
In order to arrive at that wherein thou hast no
pleasure,
Thou must go by a way wherein thou hast no
pleasure.
In order to arrive at that which thou knowest not,
Thou must go by a way that thou knowest not.
In order to arrive at that which thou possessest
not.
Thou must go by a way that thou possessest not.
In order to arrive at that which thou art not,
Thou must go through that which thou art not.

Saint John of the Cross (1542-1591)
translated by E. Allison Peers

When thy mind dwells upon anything,
Thou art ceasing to cast thyself upon the All.
For in order to pass from the all to the All,
Thou hast to deny thyself wholly in all.
And, when thou comest to possess it wholly,
Thou must possess it without desiring anything.
For, if thou wilt have anything in having all,
Thou hast not thy treasure purely in God.

Saint John of the Cross (1542-1591),
translated by E. Allison Peers

Have mercy
Upon us.
Have mercy
Upon our efforts,
That we
Before thee,
In love and in faith,
Righteousness and humility,
May follow thee,
With self-denial, steadfastness and courage,
And meet thee
In the silence.
Give us
A pure heart
That we may see thee,
A humble heart
That we may hear thee,
A heart of love
That we may serve thee,
A heart of faith
That we may live thee.
Thou
Whom I do not know
But whose I am.
Thou
Whom I do not comprehend
But who hast dedicated me
To my fate.
Thou—

Dag Hammarskjold

O Lord, how wonderful you are!
Your greatness and love overwhelms me.
You catch and hold me in your shining darkness.
You take me out of myself into the light of your
being which blinds me with its brightness.
You fill me with yourself, and my being is suffused
with the beauty of your glory.
I am speechless, silent, held by your over-
whelming love.
Lord, never let me go, keep me hidden in your-
self, always.

Etta Gullick

God is true rest. It is his will that we should know
him, and his pleasure that we should rest in him.
Nothing less will satisfy us. No soul can rest until
it is detached from all creation. When it is deliberately so detached for love of him who is all,
then only can it experience spiritual rest. So the
soul touched by the Holy Spirit prays in this kind
of way: 'God, of your goodness give me yourself,
for you are sufficient for me. I cannot properly ask
anything less, to be worthy of you. If I were to ask
less, I should always be in want. In you alone do I
have all.'

Lady Julian of Norwich

Deep and silent and cool as a broad, still, tree-
shaded river
Is the peace of thy presence, thou rest of our souls.
From the thousand problems of this our hurrying
life

We turn, with silent joy, to plunge in thee,
To steep our souls in thy quiet depths
Where no clamour of earth disturbs our perfect
content.
Thou art our home and refuge;
In thee we are safe and at peace:
Ever in the din and hurry of the world
We know that thou art near,
We know that close at hand—closer than our little
life—
Floweth that silent river of thy presence and love.
In a moment we may be with thee and in thee,
In a moment be surrounded and soaked in thy
peace:
In a moment, as this loud world clangs round us,
We may rest secure in the bliss of thine eternity.

J. S. Hoyland

My dear sister, from what I see, you desire to lose
yourself in God. To be lost in God is nothing else
than to be absolutely and completely resigned and
surrendered into his hands, and abandoned to the
care of his adorable providence. This saying 'to lose
oneself in God', has a certain substance in it that I
do not think can be fully understood unless they are
thus happily lost. The great Saint Paul fully understood it when he said with such assurance: 'I live,
yet no longer in myself, but it is Jesus Christ who
liveth in me'. How happy we should be if we could
truly say: 'It is no longer I that live in myself
because my whole life is lost in God, and it is he

171

who lives for me and in me'. To live no longer in ourselves, but lost in God, is the most sublime perfection a soul can reach. We ought to long for it, losing ourselves again and again in the ocean of that infinite greatness. But a soul thus lost is always annihilated before God; it is always content with what God does in it or outside it. Everything that happens satisfies it; affliction pleases it, and it beholds it without confusion because it will say: I have lost all consolation in that of being lost in God.

Saint Jane de Chantal (1572-1641)

Thou, O eternal Trinity, art a deep sea, into which the deeper I enter the more I find, and the more I find the more I seek; the soul cannot be satiated in thy abyss, for she continually hungers after thee, the eternal Trinity, desiring to see thee with the light of thy light. As the hart desires the springs of living water, so my soul desires to leave the prison of this dark body and see thee in truth. O abyss, O eternal Godhead, O sea profound, what more couldst thou give me than thyself? Thou art the fire that ever burns without being consumed; thou consumest in thy heat all the soul's self-love; thou art the fire which takes away cold; with thy light thou dost illuminate me so I may know all thy truth. Clothe me, clothe me, with thyself, eternal truth, so I may run this mortal life with true obedience, and with the light of thy most holy faith.

Saint Catherine of Siena (1347-1386)

Contemplation is knowing without manner,
Which remains always above reason;
It cannot descend into reason;
And reason cannot ascend to it.
The bright ignorance of manner is a fair mirror
Where God shines his eternal splendour.
The absence of manner ignores all ways of acting,
All acts of reason fall below it.
But the ignorance of manner is not God,
Rather it is the light in which we see him.
Those who live in this ignorance, in the divine light,
See in themselves a desert.
The ignorance of manner surpasses reason without
    suppressing it;
It sees all things without astonishment.
To be astonished is far beneath it,
The contemplative life is without astonishment.
In the ignorance of manner one sees but without
    knowing what is seen,
For it surpasses all and is neither this nor that.

Jan Ruysbroeck (1293-1381)

Martha is troubled, peace hath Mary. Praised is
Martha, but more Mary. Mary hath but one intention in her, and that only one intent maketh her have
peace, and Martha in many intentions, hath oft time
unrest. And therefore a free soul may only have one
intention. She heareth oft, this soul, things that she
heareth not, and is full oft times where this soul is
not, and feeleth oft times that which she feeleth not.
'I hold', saith she, 'for this, mine own which I

173

shall not let go; it is in my will, befall what may; for he is with me, then it were a default if I let myself be dismayed'.

'Mirror of Simple Souls'
(probably 13th century)

Those who approach the Lord should make their prayer in a state of quietness, of peace and great tranquility without uneasy and confused cries but by applying their attention to the Lord by the effort of the heart and the soberness of their thoughts.

Sixth Homily from Pseudo-Macarius
(4th/5th century)

Just as when the body is working at something, it applies itself wholly engrossed to its work, and all its members lend one another mutual aid—in the same way the soul should be wholly and entirely strip itself for prayer and love of Christ, being no longer agitated and scattered by its thoughts, but attaching itself with its whole expectation to Christ.

Thirty-second Homily from Pseudo-Macarius
(4th/5th century)

The summary of all good activity, the highest of our work is perseverance in prayer. By it, we may each day acquire all the virtues by asking them from God. Prayer procures for those who are judged worthy of it communion in the holiness of God, in the energy of the Spirit, and the union of the whole awareness of the spirit with the Lord in an ineffable love. He who each day forces himself to persevere in prayer is consumed by the spiritual love of a divine *eros* (love) and of a burning desire for God, and he receives the grace of sanctifying perfection.

Fortieth Homily from Pseudo-Macarius
(4th/5th century)

To be there before you, Lord, that's all.
To shut the eyes of my body,
To shut the eyes of my soul,
And to be still and silent,
To expose myself to you who are there, exposed to
me.
To be there before you, the Eternal Presence.
I am willing to feel nothing, Lord,
          to see nothing
          to hear nothing.
Empty of all ideas,
          of all images,
In the darkness.
Here I am, simply
To meet you without obstacles,
In the silence of faith,
Before you, Lord.
But Lord, I am not alone
I can no longer be alone.
I am a crowd, Lord,
For men live within me.
I have met them,
They have come in,

They have settled down,
They have worried me,
They have tormented me,
They have devoured me,
And I have allowed it, Lord, that they might be
   nourished and refreshed.
I bring them to you, too, as I come before you.
I expose them to you in exposing myself to you.
Here I am,
Here they are,
Before you, Lord.

Michel Quoist

XI

THE ONE WHO LISTENS

And so the love story of God and your soul goes on. More and more, you will experience what I am haltingly trying to express.

Every mode of being will be touched and still there will be more—because God is love, is infinite.

Do not stop loving or you will stop living. Accept the tears, the loneliness, the waiting, the persecution—anything. It is all worthwhile, in the Inexpressible who is.

This is the One who listens. 'He who has ears to hear

Let him hear.'

INDEX OF SUBJECTS

INDEX OF AUTHORS AND SOURCES

ACKNOWLEDGMENTS

The authors and the publishers wish to express their gratitude to the following for permission to include copyright material in this book:

Friendship Press for the prayer, "O Lord, the meal is steaming before us," from *I Lie on My Mat and Pray,* edited by Fritz Pawelzik.

John Murray (Publishers), Ltd., for the prayers from *With an Eye to the Future,* by Osbert Lancaster.

E. P. Dutton & Co. for the prayers from *A Chain of Prayer Across the Ages,* by Selina Fox.

The Society for Promoting Christian Knowledge for prayers from *One Man's Prayers,* by George Appleton and *My God, My Glory,* by Eric Milner White.

Harper & Row (Publishers), Inc., for the extract from *The Divine Milieu,* by Teilhard de Chardin; the prayers from *A Plain Man's Book of Prayers,* by William Barclay, *Something Beautiful for God,* by Malcolm Muggeridge, and *Prayers of the Spirit,* by J. W. Suter.

Harcourt Brace Jovanovich, Inc., for two extracts from *Poems,* by C. S. Lewis.

The Macmillan Company for the prayers from

Letters and Papers from Prison, by Dietrich Bonhoeffer.

Abingdon Press for the prayers from *Epilogues and Prayers,* by William Barclay.

Westminster Press for the prayers from *A Kind of Praying,* by Rex Chapman.

SCM Press, Ltd., for the prayers from *Book of Prayer for Students.*

Rev. A. S. T. Fisher for the prayers from his book, *An Anthology of Prayers.*

Holt, Rinehart and Winston, Inc., for the prayers from *Are You Running With Me, Jesus?,* by Malcolm Boyd.

Edward Arnold (Publishers), Ltd., for the Rev. Christopher Campling's prayer from *Words for Worship,* by Christopher Campling and Michael Davis.

The United Society for the Propagation of the Gospel for the prayers from *Prayer is My Life,* by Margaret Dewey.

The Student Christian Movement of India for the prayer, "O God, thou who art love," from *Prayers for Young Men.*

Lawrence Verry, Inc., for the prayers from *Gitanjali,* by Rabindranath Tagore and *Fruit Gathering,* by the same author.

Viking Press, Inc., for the prayers from *Prayers*

from the Ark, by Carmen Bernos de Gaztold, translated by Rumer Godden.

A. R. Mowbray & Co., Ltd., for prayers from *The Prayer Manual,* and from *A Pilgrim's Book of Prayers* and *The Face of Love,* by Gilbert Shaw.

Darton, Longman & Todd, Ltd., for the excerpts from *Listen Pilgrim,* by Christopher William Jones.

Penguin Books, Ltd., for "God is true rest," from *Revelations of Divine Love,* by Lady Julian of Norwich, translated by Clifford Wolters.

Zondervan Publishing House for the prayers from *New Every Morning.*

Search Press, Ltd., for the excerpts from *The Spirituality of the New Testament and the Fathers,* by Louis Bouyer.

Sheed & Ward for the extracts from *Prayers,* by Michael Quoist.

Seabury Press for the prayer from *Godthoughts,* by Dick Williams.

Lutterworth Press for the prayers from *Prayers at Breakfast,* by Beryl Bye.

Dom Hubert van Zeller for the prayers which carry his name.

Professor J. C. Watson's Trust for the prayers from *Carmina Gadelica, Vol. 3,* by Alexander Carmichael, published by the Scottish Academic Press.

The Grail (England) for Psalm 129 from *The Psalms: A New Translation.*

The Literary Estate of Eleanor Hull and Chatto and Windus Ltd. for "Be Thou My Vision" from *The Poem Book of the Gael,* selected and edited by Eleanor Hull.

Oxford University Press for the prayers from *Our Bounden Duty,* by Miles L. Yates.

Geoffrey Chapman, Ltd., for the prayers from *Lord, Make Me Truly Human.*

Longman Group, Ltd., for the prayers from *A Cambridge Bede Book,* by E. Milner White.

Mrs. Hoyland and Mrs. Rachel Gilliatt for the prayers by J. S. Hoyland.

Burns & Oates, Ltd., for the extracts from *Saint John of the Cross,* translated by E. Allison Peers.

Mrs. Frances Temple for the prayer by Archbishop Temple.

Paulist/Newman Press for the prayers by Huub Oosterhuis, from *Your Word is Near.*

Hodder & Stoughton, Ltd., for the prayers from *Uncommon Prayers,* by Cecil Hunt, and *Parish Prayers,* by Frank Colquhoun.

Alfred A. Knopf for the extract by Dag Hammarskjold, from *Markings.*

The Folio Society, for the extract from *Sonnets of*

Michelangelo, translated by Elizabeth Jennings, published for its members in 1961.